Using Reading to Teach a World Language

To help your students learn a world language, don't forget the power of reading! In this practical book from Donna Spangler and John Alex Mazzante, you'll gain a variety of strategies and activities that you can use to teach students to read in a world language, boosting their comprehension, vocabulary, and fluency. Perfect for any age or proficiency level, these classroom-ready activities can easily be adapted to suit your needs.

Special features:

- A discussion of the challenges to teaching reading in the world language classroom.
- A variety of adaptable pre-reading, during-reading, and post-reading strategies and activities for students across grade levels and languages.
- Essential tips for cultivating vocabulary, fluency, and comprehension.
- Reader's Theater—a special chapter of strategies for implementing this exciting technique.
- A list of helpful websites and apps for world language teachers.
- Useful appendices, including reproducible material for your classroom.

Busy world language teachers will love this book's numerous classroom examples, ready-to-use templates, and free online reading sources. Bonus: the book includes eResources that are free to adapt and print for classroom use from our website, http://www.routledge.com/books/details/9781138853515.

Donna Spangler has taught Spanish and French at the middle school level for over 26 years. A former chair of the Derry Township School District Induction Committee, she holds an educational doctorate in Teacher Leadership from Walden University. In 2011, she was named the Pennsylvania State Modern Language Association Educator of the Year.

John Alex Mazzante teaches Spanish at the high school and middle school levels. He holds a bachelor of arts from Lycoming College with a major in Spanish. He has attended Tandem Escuela Internacional of Madrid, Spain and has completed translation work for local companies.

Using Reading to Teach a World Language

Strategies and Activities

Donna Spangler and John Alex Mazzante

Routledge
Taylor & Francis Group

NEW YORK AND LONDON

First published 2015
by Routledge
711 Third Avenue, New York, NY 10017

and by Routledge
2 Park Square, Milton Park, Abingdon, Oxon, OX14 4RN

Routledge is an imprint of the Taylor & Francis Group, an informa business

© 2015 Taylor & Francis

Portions of this book were previously published in the 2012 Pennsylvania Language Forum as articles entitled, "A Research Toolkit of 12 Reading Strategies for the Foreign Language Classroom" (pp. 5–15) and "Reader's Theater in the Foreign Language Classroom" (pp. 34–42). Used with permission. www.psmla.net/forum

Library of Congress Cataloging-in-Publication Data
Spangler, Donna.
  Using reading to teach a world language : strategies and activities / Donna Spangler and John Alex Mazzante.
      pages cm
  Includes bibliographical references and index.
  1. Reading. 2. Creative activities and seat work. 3. Language and languages—Study and teaching. I. Mazzante, John Alex. II. Title.
    LB1050.S615 2014
    428.4—dc23
    2014035793

ISBN: 978-1-138-85349-2 (hbk)
ISBN: 978-1-138-85351-5 (pbk)
ISBN: 978-1-315-72275-7 (ebk)

Typeset in Optima
by Apex CoVantage, LLC

Contents

Contents

Part 5   Reader's Theater

eResources

The templates in this book can be downloaded and printed for classroom use. You can access these downloads by visiting the book product page on our website, http://www.routledge.com/books/details/9781138853515. Then click on the tab that says "eResources," and select the files. They will begin downloading to your computer.

Here is a list of the free templates available:

1. Strategy 1: Annolighting the Text
2. Strategy 5: Bloom's Taxonomy Questions
3. Strategy 9: Five W's and an H
4. Strategy 15: KWL Chart
5. Strategy 20: Predicting ABCs
6. Strategy 23: Say, Mean, Matter
7. Strategy 26: Story Mapping
8. Strategy 28: Textbook Activity Guide (TAG)
9. Strategy 32: Three-Two-One (3-2-1)
10. Strategy 34: Vocabulary Builder
11. Strategy 35: Vocabulary Prediction Chart
12. Activity 8: Inference Boxes
13. Activity 21: Tic-Tac-Toe Choice Board

Meet the Authors

Dr. Donna Spangler is a Spanish teacher in the Derry Township School District in Hershey, PA. Prior to coming to Hershey in 1997, she taught Spanish in the Upper Darby School District. In 2009, Donna completed her EdD in Teacher Leadership. She holds a BS of Ed. in Spanish; a K–12 principal's certificate; two Master's Degrees with a specialization in curriculum, instruction, and assessment; and an Instructional Technology Integration certificate from the ACTFL program at the University of Maryland.

Currently, Dr. Spangler is the president of the Hershey Education Association in the Derry Township School District. In addition, Dr. Spangler is the editor of the Forum for the Pennsylvania State Modern Language Association (PSMLA) and a board member of that organization. In 2011, she received PSMLA's Educator of the Year: K–12 award. She is also a member of Learning Forward PA's board; the focus of that organization is the importance of effective professional learning to improve teaching, leadership, and student learning. She has published articles called "Brain-Compatible Second-Language Learning" and "Mapping the World Language Teacher Evaluation in Pennsylvania: Hopes, Facts, Challenges, and Questions."

In Derry Township, she chaired the DTSD District Induction Program from June 2001 through May 2007. She also presented that induction program at both the state and national levels through the Pennsylvania Staff Development Council conference and the National Staff Development Council conference.

John Alex Mazzante teaches Spanish at the high school and middle school levels. He holds a bachelor of arts from Lycoming College. He studied Spanish in Tandem Escuela Internacional of Madrid, Spain, and has traveled throughout the central and southern provinces of the Iberian Peninsula, as well as the Balearic Islands, Morocco, Germany, and parts of Ecuador. Currently he collaborates with the Colegio Técnico Profesional de San Joaquín de Flores of Costa Rica on a Skype pen-pal project with his high school's National Spanish Honors Society. Outside of the classroom, he has completed translation work for Power Point Technology Inc. and

Chemcoat Inc., and has also co-published multiple articles in publications for the Pennsylvania State Modern Language Association.

The co-authors of this book have also co-authored three additional published articles, called "Responsive Teaching in the Second Language Classroom: Motivating Students' Needs and Motivating Students Through Differentiated Instruction," "A Research Toolkit of 12 Reading Strategies for the Foreign Language Classroom," and "Reader's Theater in the Foreign Language Classroom."

Acknowledgments

We would like to acknowledge and to thank those who have helped us in many ways to make this published book a reality. We are both extremely grateful to Lauren Davis and Emily Greenberg from Routledge for believing in our work and giving us the opportunity to share it. Their support, energy, communication, and confidence enabled us to remain true to ourselves while helping us to share our work with fellow educators.

We also are indebted to the people whose ideas and input have made this collection possible, because this work is the result of what we have learned from our students, our colleagues, professional conferences, research, and reflections about our teaching practices.

Donna would like to express her sincere gratitude to the following people:

- My parents, Christine and Ronald Fink, for teaching me the value of a good education and giving me their gifts of Godly guidance, strength, and perseverance.
- My husband, Tom Spangler, and my sister, Sheryl Haertter, for their constant understanding and support.
- Joy Graeff, Kathy Mack, Sue McDonald, Sarah Smith, Tracie Dawson, Barb Clouser, Diane May, Connie Metzler, Althea Cirillo, and Marcia Parsons for their interest in my work and their continual encouragement.
- Dr. Aaron Shuman, the Pennsylvania State Modern Language Association (PSMLA) organization, and the Learning Forward PA (LFPA) organization, all of whom have been instrumental in my growth as an educator and as a professional over the years.
- My co-author and former colleague, John Alex Mazzante, for his expertise, collaboration, friendship, support, and humor throughout the years.

John would like to acknowledge and thank the following people:

- My father, John R. Mazzante, for instilling in me the importance of hard, honest work and my mother, Valerie Mazzante, for being a model of compassion and love.

- My older sister, Amanda, for giving me a wonderful niece, Maura, and nephew, Kane, and my younger sister, Ashley, for traveling around the world with me.
- My great uncle, Carmen Cillo, who has taught me how to have a relationship with God, my creator.
- Carolyn Hunt for her unconditional love and contagious passion for language and reading.
- Mr. Daniel D. Taormina, Mr. Chris King, Victoria Stetts, Andrea Tira, Bruce Buckle, Lynn Shirk, and Jenny Seyfert, who have inspired me along my career and have guided me throughout the teaching profession.
- My co-author and friend, Donna Spangler, for her guidance, loyalty, inspiration, and belief in me.

Preface

This book is a how-to book of reading strategies, activities, and Reader's Theater for use in the world language classroom, with many practical strategies, modifications, and adaptations for the classroom teacher. Although classroom teachers are the primary audience of this book, university professors, principals, curriculum leaders, department heads, and pre-service educators will also find this a useful guide for effective reading.

This book evolved out of a need that both authors found when they were using reading in their world language classrooms. Without a doubt, reading is one of the best ways to incorporate target language input into a world language classroom. Common Core State Standards, standardized testing, and ACTFL proficiency targets have increased the emphasis on reading instruction in the last few years.

However, even though world language teachers realize there are many benefits to increasing reading in their classrooms, many teachers also feel acutely the challenges introduced by such. Some teachers are uncertain of what reading strategies and activities to use other than translation activities and a question-and-answer session at the end of a reading. Other teachers worry about how to encourage whole-text reading in the target language by students, rather than students going "dictionary diving." Other teachers don't feel they have a variety of strategies and activities at their fingertips to assess for understanding throughout the reading process.

As teachers, we both felt that reading in the target language was something we both wanted to incorporate more effectively into our classrooms, and we both began to collaborate together on ways we could improve reading use for second language (L2) students. This book is the culmination of what we have used as strategies and activities in our classrooms to improve the quality of our instruction. We began with the intention of collecting a few ideas for ourselves to share with each other about reading that we "road-tested" in our classrooms so that we weren't using the same activities or ideas over and over again. It grew beyond our original intentions to what you will now find in this book.

This book is divided into several sections.

Part 1: "Reading in the World Language Classroom" outlines the benefits to adding reading to a world language classroom, and explains why reading is not an easy task for teachers and students.

Part 2: "Implications for L2 Teachers" explains how to cultivate strategic L2 readers with regard to vocabulary, fluency, and comprehension instruction in the world language classroom. This overview also gives explanations in planning "pre-reading," "during-reading," and "post-reading" strategies and activities.

Part 3: "Reading Strategies" incorporates the research and theoretical background of L2 reading into 37 actual reading assessments, and identifies which strategies the teacher can use before reading, during reading, and after reading tasks in the classroom.

Part 4: "Reading Activities" uses the research and theoretical background of L2 reading in 26 different reading activities, and identifies which strategies the teacher can use before reading, during reading, and after reading tasks in the classroom.

Part 5: "Reader's Theater" explains the benefits of this activity in the L2 classroom with four different ways teachers can do this activity in the classroom. Twenty-five additional suggestions are then given to add more interest and variety to Reader's Theater in the L2 classroom.

Part 6: "Resources, References, and Downloads" contains 19 online resources, a list of references, and 13 free downloads for classroom teachers.

We sincerely hope that you find the strategies and activities in this book to be useful and time-saving as you decide what to use with your students. Remember, if a strategy or activity doesn't exactly match the language level or grade of your students, you can always adjust the content or the strategy/activity to better meet the language and reading level of your students.

Reading in the World Language Classroom

Introduction

Stephen Krashen, an expert linguist in second language acquisition and founder of the current theory of language acquisition, asserted in his book, *The Power of Reading* (2004), that reading "is the way to achieve advanced second language proficiency. It is one of the best things a second language acquirer can do to bridge the gap from beginning level to truly advanced levels of language proficiency" (p. x). In recent years, there has been considerable interest in promoting reading as a significant means of language development for first and second language learners, along with many research studies demonstrating the benefits with regard to language development for world language students (Day & Bamford, 1998; Krashen, 1995).

Many research studies have shown that second language (L2) students can acquire many benefits when reading L2 material for L2 learning (Elley, 1989; 1991; Hafiz & Tudor, 1990; Nation, 1997; Tsang, 1996). These studies cite the benefits of L2 as recorded in measures of oral language, reading comprehension, vocabulary use and knowledge, and L2 writing. These improvements are attributed to various reading studies in which students received L2 input of meaningful print through L2 reading. Krashen and McQuillan (2007) explain, "Studies confirm that students who do L2 reading can read better, write better, spell better, have better grammatical competence, and have larger vocabulary in the target language" (p. 68). As a result of the success of these research studies and in the interest in improving L2 instruction in the limited time that L2 teachers have with their students in the classroom, there has been a push in recent years to add or increase the reading component in L2 classrooms.

Benefits to Adding Reading to the L2 Classroom

Many world language teachers, both experienced and novice, are looking for ways to tackle the very complex and challenging task of teaching reading to their students in an L2 classroom. Increasing the amount and types of reading materials available in an L2 classroom allows teachers to not only add worthwhile content input materials for their students but, depending upon what types of reading a teacher chooses to add, even increase students' access to authentic culture and materials. There are many benefits to adding or increasing the reading being done in the L2 classroom. Some reasons include:

- Reading has a communicative value and functions as an active skill, because cognitive processes are working during reading.
- The design of meaningful exercises will lead to assist communication between the reader and the writer or the reader and the teacher.
- Reading comprehension activities can suit the chosen texts.
- A wide variety of activities can take place using reading.
- Reading increases available language input for the students.
- Students can read a variety of author's styles of writing and text types.
- Teachers can incorporate culture through reading.
- Reading can enhance students' L2 vocabulary.
- Reading engages higher levels of cognitive thinking through systematic practice, such as students' ability to infer information.

The purpose of L2 reading is to make meaning from language written in the text. In L2 classrooms, teachers want L2 students to progress from learning to read toward reading to learn. The access to text variety, information, and authentic realia that L2 reading affords to the world language student is not easily duplicated through any other means of L2 instruction. Cultivating an atmosphere of L2 reading in a world language classroom is a goal of many L2 teachers.

L2 Teachers Are Often Ill-Prepared or Unprepared to Teach Reading in L2

Although there are many benefits to increasing reading in a second language classroom, L2 teachers are often uncertain about how to go about doing this in their classrooms. Many teachers have few tools in their teaching toolbox to implement L2 reading effectively. Most L2 teachers have had little to no training in how to teach and how to incorporate L2 reading into their classrooms. As a result, there is a gap between L2 classroom instructional practices and consistent, systemic L2 literacy development.

Some L2 teachers completed only a single course in reading methods at the university level while other L2 teachers report that their methodology course outlines didn't even provide such a course to prospective L2 teachers. As a result, many L2 teacher preparation programs failed to adequately prepare their teacher candidates to teach reading. In addition, L2 teachers often report that little L2 professional development is provided to teachers in the form of in-service professional development at their current schools.

As a result, many L2 teachers may be unaware of effective, research-based strategies and activities that they can implement in their L2 classrooms to increase world language students' vocabulary, fluency, and comprehension of the text. Because these teachers have little background in reading, L2 teachers often resort instead to three basic reading strategies: teaching vocabulary in a decontextualized fashion, translating the world language text into English, and asking summative comprehension questions at the end of the text piece or chapter.

However, there are a myriad of other strategies and activities that L2 teachers can incorporate into their classrooms through systematic practice to increase students' decoding abilities and to deepen students' comprehension of the selected text. Strategy training, therefore, is an important skill in developing students' L2 reading skills. It is important, though, that L2 strategy training be seen by L2 teachers as something to be done over an extended period of time and to be implemented consistently. It is not to be used as a "one-time" vaccination in the L2 classroom. To be done effectively, L2 reading strategies need to be consistently taught and used by the L2 teacher for maximum effectiveness.

Why We Wrote This Book

Our goal in writing this book is to help world language students become engaged, fluent, and competent readers of both academic and recreational texts in the L2 target language and to help world language teachers utilize various strategies and activities to make L2 text more meaningful and interactive for the student. We want to provide a variety of strategies that L2 teachers can use with their students to help them become more effective readers and independent learners in a second language. This book is designed to be a resource to assist teachers in expanding their current repertoire of reading strategies. It does not prescribe one "best" method or model of teaching L2 reading to students. Rather, its purpose is to serve as a resource for L2 teachers as they consider their curriculum requirements, the needs of their students, the levels of their students, and their own unique teaching styles.

In this book, we . . .

- Provide practical strategies that L2 teachers can add to their current L2 reading repertoire
- Outline ideas and activities that teachers can use with a variety of text types
- Share research evidence related to the cognitive perspective of reading
- Encourage teachers to adapt and to extend the ideas presented in this book to develop successful practices for developing stronger L2 readers

Teaching Reading is *Not* an Easy Task

Wren (n.d.) cited as number one in his top 10 myths influencing present-day reading instruction the idea that "learning to read is a natural process" (p. 1). Wren stated (n.d.),

> It has long been argued that learning to read, like learning to understand spoken language, is a natural phenomenon. It has often been suggested that children will learn to read if they are simply immersed in a literacy-rich environment and allowed to develop literacy skills in their own way. This belief that learning to read is a natural process that comes from rich text experiences is surprisingly prevalent in education despite the fact that learning to read is about as natural as learning to juggle blindfolded while riding a unicycle backwards. Simply put, learning to read is not only unnatural, it is just about the most unnatural thing humans do.
>
> (p. 1)

Moats (1999) concurred: "Contrary to the popular theory that learning to read is natural and easy, learning to read is a complex linguistic achievement. For many children, it requires effort and incremental skill development" (p. 11). Reading, unlike speech, is an unnatural act and children should not be expected to learn to read without explicit instruction (Adams & Bruck, 1993; Liberman, 1992).

But perhaps the most compelling information that demonstrates that reading is not an easy task is the statistics that show a prevalent literacy gap that exists in America, which is not limited to any one segment of the population. In an executive summary of the report *Teaching Reading IS Rocket Science,* Moats (1999) shared:

- Approximately 20 per cent of elementary students nationwide have significant problems reading.
- At least 20 per cent of elementary students do not read fluently enough to engage in independent reading.
- The rate of reading failure is approximately 60 to 70 per cent for African-American, Hispanic, limited-English speakers, and poor children.
- Approximately one-third of poor readers in America are from college-educated families.
- Twenty-five per cent of adults in the United States lack basic literacy skills required in a typical job (p. 7).

Therefore, the idea of many L2 teachers that the only thing that L2 teachers need to do is to provide L2 reading materials to their students in order for them to become effective and proficient L2 readers is not accurate. L2 teachers need to do more than simply make an L2 literary environment accessible to their students;

L2 teachers need to strategically plan, implement, and teach L2 reading strategies. These L2 reading strategies need to be more sophisticated than the three main strategies many L2 teachers rely on: giving students lists of vocabulary words to memorize before reading, translating the L2 text into English, and asking summative comprehension questions at the end of a text piece or chapter.

Reading Is Complex

Years ago, reading was regarded by teachers and researchers as simply a receptive skill. It was considered a passive way for students to acquire information. However, recent research findings both in the areas of reading and brain-based research have found the contrary. What may look to someone watching a reader as a passive process is actually a very active process within the brain, involving a large array of cognitive processes.

According to the Southwest Educational Development Laboratory there are 14 cognitive processes involved in reading acquisition. These include: reading comprehension, language comprehension, background, linguistic, phonology, syntax, semantics, decoding, cipher, lexical, phoneme, alphabetic, letter, and concepts. Because 14 cognitive processes are used, reading is the result of a very complex process within the brain. World language teachers should not be surprised that teaching reading in a second language is a difficult skill for students to do well.

Reading Proficiency Is Dependent

Reading comprehension and reading proficiency are equally dependent on two critical skills: language comprehension, which is the ability to construct meaning from the language the text is written in, and decoding, which is the ability to recognize and to process words in the text. Both language comprehension and decoding are necessary for reading comprehension (Hoover & Gough, n.d.; Snow, Burns, & Griffin, 1998). Students who readily understand spoken language and who are able to fluently and easily recognize printed words do not have problems with reading comprehension. However, students must be proficient in BOTH domains to do well. Difficulty with EITHER language comprehension or decoding will result in poor reading comprehension.

Implications for L2 Teachers

With reading, world language teachers deal with a double-edged sword. First, in order for students to achieve reading acquisition, students must have sufficient language comprehension and a strong decoding ability within the target language. Since reading relies heavily on previously acquired spoken language, world language students can be at a disadvantage depending upon what they are being asked to read in the L2 target language. For some students, their spoken language ability may be limited at a beginning, emergent, or intermediate level. As a result, depending upon the reading activity, reading can be challenging to limited-language students.

In addition, don't forget that statistics show that many students experience reading difficulties within their primary language. As stated earlier, research has shown that reading involves 14 cognitive processes in the brain. Because of the many steps involved in reading, challenges can occur for students anywhere within these processes. Sousa (2001) explained, "Reading . . . requires the learning of specific skills that are not innate to brain functions" (p. 205). Depending upon how well or how poorly students can utilize reading skills also contributes to their success or frustration when reading in L2. These difficulties do not suddenly disappear when a student tries to read in a second language. Any primary language reading difficulties continue to provide challenges for students reading in a second language.

Cultivating Strategic L2 Readers

If reading isn't an easy or natural skill and requires a multitude of cognitive processes, teachers need to explicitly teach strategies to help students construct meaning as they read. Hoping that all students somehow intuitively learn how to effectively approach the complex task of reading simply doesn't happen for most students out of thin air or by magic. Reading isn't a passive activity where students decode words on a page. Instead, reading is an active process where students construct meaning and have an active role to play while reading. Sherman (1991) explained that reading transcended the mere transmission of information by fostering an imaginative dialogue between the text and the reader's mind to actually help people to think.

Effective readers are strategic. Good readers interact with the text. They construct meaning, make predictions, organize information, evaluate reading information, connect ideas to prior knowledge, monitor their comprehension, and know how to make adjustments when they have problems understanding what they are reading. During the process of reading, there is an important interaction that occurs between the author's written words, the student's language, the student's thoughts, and the student's background knowledge. As a result, world language teachers need to be aware of ways to enhance students' ability to read for comprehension. Without comprehension, reading for a student becomes an empty and meaningless task.

There is a large body of research that provides substantial evidence that explicit reading and comprehension instruction improves students' understanding of texts and that when researchers or teachers explicitly taught the students comprehension strategies, the students were able to not only apply the strategies but also improve their overall comprehension (Block & Pressley, 2002; Block, Gambrell, & Pressley, 2002; National Reading Panel, 2000; Ruddell & Unrau, 2004). Teachers who give students explicit instruction in reading strategies help students to be more skillful and strategic readers. A strategic reader is a reader who understands when and how to use a strategy to help him or her comprehend a text. While some students use strategies intuitively during the reading process, most students need to be taught how to use the strategies and how to actively think during reading.

By carefully scaffolding and monitoring students' interactions with various texts, teachers help students become better readers. Well-designed strategy lessons should support students as they move from the literal text level (i.e., information stated directly in the reading) to the inferential level (i.e., information implied in the text or connections with the reader's personal background knowledge) and finally to the metacognitive level (i.e., students reflecting on their own thinking and learning). Teaching reading strategies to students is effective because the strategies encourage development of text representations that might not develop in the absence of instruction (Pressley & Wharton-McDonald, 1997).

Developing Strategic Reading Activities

When a teacher develops strategic reading activities, it involves more than just choosing a text that is at the right level for students, writing a set of comprehension questions for students to answer after reading, and having the students work on the reading assignment. Richardson and Morgan (1994) developed a framework for strategic teaching that they call "**PAR**." The acronym stands for: **P**reparation and planning before reading, **A**ssistance and associations during reading, and

Reflection and readiness for application after reading. A fully developed strategic reading activity supports the students as they read through pre-reading, during-reading, and post-reading activities.

As an L2 teacher develops strategic reading activities, there are several things the teacher may wish to keep in mind:

1. *Construct reading activities around a purpose.* Just as an architect doesn't begin to design a building without first knowing the purpose for the building and how it will be used, so too should L2 language teachers consider the purpose for the reading before designing reading activities around it. There are many purposes for reading: a teacher may want the students to understand the main idea of the reading, recount the gist of the story, identify specific information within the reading, describe the characters of the reading, evaluate the reading, add their own interpretation to the reading, continue the story, or simply enjoy the reading.

2. *Select a text that is at the appropriate level for the students.* Teachers should assess the ease or difficulty level of a text for the group of students. In addition, teachers should consider how much background knowledge students have (or will need to have) to comprehend the topic, the type of text it is (i.e., narrative, informative, persuasive), and the amount of visual pictures available to the students (i.e., drawings, photographs, maps) that will help students with unfamiliar words and to check their own comprehension of the text.

3. *Determine the instruction goal(s) for the activities.* In addition to determining the purpose for the text reading, the teacher may consider if there are additional instructional goals to highlight. Some goals might include: previewing content information, understanding cultural content, practicing or reviewing grammatical structures, introducing new vocabulary, reinforcing previous vocabulary, or familiarizing students with text structure.

4. *Identify pre-reading activities to prepare students for successful reading of the text.* The activities in the "pre-reading" section should be structured with the intention of helping to introduce the students to the upcoming text, to elicit or to provide appropriate background knowledge, and helping students to approach the L2 text in a more meaningful and purposeful manner while increasing students' interest.

5. *Select during-reading activities that match the purpose for reading and highlight the instructional goals for the reading.* The activities in the "during-reading" section should be designed to help students develop purposeful reading strategies, improve their control of the L2 text, and decode L2 text passages. These activities should help the students and the teacher to check students' comprehension as they read.

6. *Identify post-reading activities that demonstrate understanding of the reading and/or extend the learning.* "Post-reading" activities should help to check

students' comprehension and then lead the students to a deeper analysis of the text, or otherwise extend their learning. By reviewing the text information again, students can focus on information they didn't comprehend fully or didn't comprehend correctly, resulting in deeper text analysis.

Planning "Pre-Reading" Strategies or Activities

Many times teachers forget about the importance of providing students with pre-reading strategies or activities. Instead, teachers focus on presenting the actual reading content but do little to prepare students to read the text assignments or comprehend what they will read (Wood & Muth, 1991). Buehl (1995) referred to pre-reading activities as "frontloading" and asserted that by providing students with meaningful pre-reading activities, teachers not only increased students' readiness to learn but also fostered strategic reading.

There are a variety of reasons to use pre-reading strategies or activities. Through pre-reading, the L2 teacher may want to:

- Assess students' background knowledge of the text
- Activate students' background knowledge of the text so students can connect that knowledge with what they will read in the text
- Provide students with the background knowledge needed to comprehend the upcoming text
- Discuss the author, story, or text type
- Consider visual illustrations, drawings, diagrams, or maps
- Predict text content
- Increase students' interest and motivate students to read the text
- Clarify cultural information to help students understand the text
- Make students aware of the purpose for reading
- Help students to navigate the type of text they will be reading
- Provide an opportunity for group or collaborative work
- Promote class discussion about the upcoming reading
- Teach skimming and scanning techniques
- Provide any language preparation needed to successfully read the text
- Highlight new vocabulary found in the text

Planning "During-Reading" Strategies or Activities

In during-reading activities, the students and the teacher check comprehension as they read. Watching how students read and how students react to reading is important to determine if students comprehend the text or not. Clay (2002) stated that observation of students' reading gives teachers "information needed to design sound instruction" (p. 11). The purpose for reading determines the type of activities a teacher should target and teach the students during classroom instruction. As students actively process what they read, it is not a neatly linear process. Instead, students engage in a "start-pause" nature of the learning process in which the following activities can occur in any order: monitoring comprehension, adjusting progress, reviewing material for clarification, developing a mental summary of what was read, and comparing current knowledge with previous knowledge (Jones, Palincsar, Ogle, & Carr, 1987).

The during-reading activities are designed in such a way as to help students develop deliberate reading strategies, improve their grasp of the L2 text, and decode L2 text passages. There are a variety of reasons to use during-reading strategies or activities. During reading, the L2 teacher may want to:

- Draw attention to word formation clues
- Read for specific pieces of information
- Distinguish between cognates and false cognates
- React to texts with summaries
- Make predictions
- Summarize text content
- Clarify and comprehend text content
- Identify and use visual reading aids
- Understand the story line/sequence of ideas
- Restate main ideas
- Interact with the text through directions and questions
- Understand the writer's purpose and intention
- Recognize the text structure and text organization
- Discover cross-cultural differences in reading
- Find the answers to pre-reading questions

Planning "Post-Reading" Strategies or Activities

Learning a second language takes hundreds and hundreds of contact hours, along with knowing thousands and thousands of words. White, Graves, and Slater (1990) determined that in a student's first language, most students had a vocabulary of around 5,800 words. They discovered that disadvantaged students had around 2,900 vocabulary words or less (in the student's first language). According to Derin and Gokce (2006), research indicated that reading is important to language and vocabulary learning but that it should be supplemented with post-reading activities in order to increase students' vocabulary knowledge.

Students have a better chance of retaining information if they actually *use* the information rather than simply read it. This holds true for vocabulary acquisition. Vocabulary that is actually used by the student results in a greater chance of the student retaining the vocabulary than if they simply read it. In addition, post-reading activities help to check students' comprehension of the text and then lead the students to a deeper analysis of the text. By reviewing the text information again, students can identify information and interpretations they understood from the text and focus on information they didn't comprehend or didn't comprehend correctly, resulting in deeper text analysis.

There are a variety of reasons to use post-reading strategies or activities. Regarding post-reading activities, the L2 teacher may want to:

- Reenact text
- Dramatize interviews based on the text
- Transfer the reading content to other types of written or spoken work
- Make connections
- Extend the reading experience
- Cement the learning from the pre-reading and during-reading activities
- Lead students into a deeper analysis of the text or meaning of the reading
- Use information in classroom games
- Review target vocabulary words and structures
- Review critical questions and comprehension of the text

The Goal: Teaching Students to Use the Strategies and Activities Independently

It is important to note that use of strategic reading instruction by the teacher is not the teacher's final goal. Ultimately, the goal of strategic reading instruction is for the students to independently access and use the strategies. It is critical that teachers overtly instruct the students about how and why they are using various techniques so that students can metacognitively reflect and recognize which strategies help them when reading. Through the teacher using a systematic, organized approach to reading, students can practice the strategies to the point that they become natural to use when reading on their own. As teachers, we want our students to develop ultimately into independent learners rather than remaining dependent learners. This teacher goal can have a significant impact on getting students to develop into lifelong learners and become lifelong readers.

Scaffolding instruction focuses on how students learn (Collins, Brown, & Newman, 1989). Pearson and Gallagher (1983) developed a scaffolding framework called the gradual release of responsibility. In this concept, the teacher first models the skill or strategy. Then the teacher gives support through sharing and guidance while the students are learning the new skill or strategy. Over time, the teacher's support and direction decreases as the students gain responsibility for their own learning and use of the skill or strategy. In this framework, the teacher moves from modeling the skill to sharing and guiding students as they practice the skill; finally, students should be able to independently apply the skill. Throughout this process, it is important that the teacher demonstrates and explains the use of the strategies in a metacognitive manner.

Being able to read well is a skill that is built on in stages through an ongoing process. As students become strategic readers, they move through four stages of reading: emergent, early, transitional, and fluent (Ellery, 2005). As the teacher, it is important to select strategies and activities that meet the purpose for reading and that the teacher tailors to meet the current reading stage of his/her students. Careful design for the instruction should move students from observing teacher modeling of the activity or strategy, to the teacher guiding and supporting students as they work on the activity or strategy, to students independently using the strategy over time.

Vocabulary Instruction

A large body of literature has touted reading as the main source of students' vocabulary development (Cunningham & Stanovich, 2003; Krashen, 1989; Nagy & Herman, 1985; 1987). Billmeyer and Barton (1998) stated, "Research conducted in the past ten years reveals that vocabulary knowledge is the single most important factor contributing to reading comprehension" (p. 19). Vocabulary knowledge heavily influences both reading fluency and reading comprehension (Robb, 1997). A student's vocabulary size is a good predictor of the student's reading comprehension (Langenberg, 2000; Rosenshine, 1980). Reading is the single most important factor in increasing students' word knowledge (Anderson & Nagy, 1991; Baumann & Kameenui, 1991).

In a student's first language, five- to six-year-olds have a vocabulary of 2,500 to 5,000 words (Beck & McKeown, 1991). The typical student learns about 3,000 words per year in the early school years at a rate of about eight words per day during the entire year (Baumann & Kameenui, 1991; Beck & McKeown, 1991; Graves, 1986). In addition, the more storybook reading a child experiences during the preschool years, the larger the child's vocabulary and language development (Sulzby & Teale, 1991). Students learning their first language acquire the majority of their large vocabularies by 12th grade and the estimate of the size of their vocabulary ranges between 40,000 (Nagy & Herman, 1987) and 80,000 words (Anderson, 1996; Anderson & Nagy, 1992), depending upon what is considered a word. In a world language classroom, if a student were to learn eight new vocabulary words per day in 180 days, the students would learn 1,440 words in a typical school year.

In a world language class, there is no doubt that students need various opportunities to learn and develop a rich vocabulary through a variety of ways like reading, writing, listening, and speaking. If students do not understand a significant portion of the vocabulary they are encountering, they often cannot understand what they are reading. If students do not know the meaning of the words they read, the reading process becomes meaningless decoding (Pinnell & Fountas, 1998). Limited vocabulary is the primary limiting factor for reading success (Becker, 1977).

A variety of approaches for increasing vocabulary is more effective than a single method (Graves, 1986). Approaches might include associations, contextualized clues, categorizations, visual images, nonlinguistic representations, word awareness, and extended reading practice. Incorporating vocabulary instruction into an L2 lesson should encourage students to make connections to new and already known words, discuss meanings of new words, apply new words, think strategically about the vocabulary, and provide multiple exposure and re-exposure to the target vocabulary.

Although research clearly indicates that teachers should use a variety of approaches to teach vocabulary in their classrooms, many teachers simply have students look up the meaning of words in textbook glossaries or dictionaries to memorize word meanings. This method, though widely used, is not effective in the long term as the vocabulary does not transfer into students' everyday language (Billmeyer & Barton, 1998). Using a dictionary does not always improve students' comprehension (Koyama & Takeuchi, 2004) and a concern among researchers is that the time it takes for a student to look up a word in a dictionary interferes with the readers' short-term memory, detracting from the student focusing on the text as a whole (Knight, 1994).

In addition, there is disagreement among researchers as to whether vocabulary is better taught *before* students read the text that contains the vocabulary or whether vocabulary should be taught *while* students are reading the text passages. Some studies have shown that intensive pre-teaching of vocabulary improves comprehension (Laflamme, 1997). Ajideh (2006) asserted, "Students are more likely to experience success with reading if they are familiar with selected vocabulary items before they begin reading" (p. 3). Other studies have demonstrated that helping students to acquire information and vocabulary while reading the text improves students' learning (Armbruster & Nagy, 1992).

There is also disagreement as to whether *narrow reading* or *extensive reading* better develops students' vocabulary. Advocates of narrow reading believe that linguistic characteristics of authentic reading materials help students' vocabulary exposure and recycling in the reading curricula of both a first language or the study of a second language (Cho, Ahn, & Krashen, 2005; Day, 1994; Krashen, 2004; Schmitt & Carter, 2000). Through narrow reading, advocates believe that world language readers will receive repetitive, comprehensible input needed for language acquisition. Nation (1997) explained:

Essentially, vocabulary learning from extensive reading is very fragile. If the small amount of learning of a word is not soon reinforced by another meeting, then that learning will be lost. It is thus critically important in an extensive reading program that learners have the opportunity to keep meeting words they have met before.

(p. 15)

Proponents of extensive reading believe that students will experience new words multiple times in varied contexts during extensive reading, resulting in "incidental acquisition" of new vocabulary (Nagy, 1997; Nagy, Anderson, & Herman, 1987; Nagy & Herman, 1987; Shu, Anderson, & Zhang, 1995). This learning is called incidental because it is a by-product rather than the main purpose for reading (Day, Omura, & Hiramatsu, 1991; Pigada & Schmitt, 2006; Waring & Takaki, 2003). Coady (1997) claimed that extensive reading leads to "greater vocabulary growth than any program of explicit instruction alone ever could" (p. 225). Day and Barnford (2002) identified 10 principles of extensive reading: the reading material is easy; a variety of reading material on a wide range of topics must be available; learners choose what to read; learners read as much as possible; the purpose for reading is pleasure, information, and general understanding; reading is its own reward; reading speed is usually faster than slower; reading is individual and silent; teachers orient and guide their students; and the teacher is the role model of a reader (pp. 137–140).

Although vocabulary acquisition occurs primarily through spoken input for a child's first language, in a world language environment vocabulary acquisition often occurs more through written text (Grabe, 2004). Empirical studies in world language have resulted in conflicting research results and have not definitively determined if vocabulary learned through instruction or vocabulary learned incidentally results in more effective language acquisition (Pigada & Schmitt, 2006). Until the research becomes clearer in this area, it may be prudent for world language teachers to implement both narrow reading and extended reading into their classroom repertoire.

Fluency Instruction

Research has determined that cognitive reading strategies, metacognitive reading strategies, schemata, and fluency all play critical roles in constructing meaning from text. The National Reading Panel report defined fluency as "the ability to read a text quickly, accurately, and with proper expression" (National Reading Panel, 2000, p. 3-1). In a study conducted by Pinnell et al. (1995), it was reported that students who performed poorly on fluency measures also tended to have low comprehension scores. According to Fuchs, Fuchs, Hosp, and Jenkins (2001), the acquisition of good fluency strategies is critical to students' comprehension and important to students' reading proficiency.

There has been extensive research on reading in a first language that shows the critical role that fluency has in successful reading. Although the skill of fluency alone does not guarantee a successful reader, research indicates that a good reading ability is virtually impossible in the absence of fast and accurate word recognition skills and fluency (Taguchi, Takayasu-Maass, & Gorsuch, 2004).

When readers use all their efforts to decode unknown text words, they begin to lose meaning about what they are reading. "Becoming a fluent reader has as much to do with constructing meaning as it has to do with attending to words on a page" (Forbes & Briggs, 2003, p. 3). Research indicates that the brain can devote only a limited amount of attention to any given cognitive task (LaBerge & Samuels, 1974; Sousa, 2001). Skillful readers in second language and world language contexts carry out word recognition tasks automatically, allowing them to devote most of their cognitive resources to comprehending the text (Anderson, 1999; Day & Bamford, 1998; Grabe, 1991). The automaticity theory is at the crux of understanding reading fluency. According to this theory, two steps are involved to get meaning from printed text: decoding and comprehension.

There are a variety of fluency tools that a world language teacher can add to his or her toolbox. Fluency skills are linked to students' comprehension and ensure higher reading proficiency. These strategies include phrasing, assisted reading, and rereading or repeated reading.

Phrasing is the skill of reading several words together, giving meaning to an appropriate text phrase rather than word-by-word reading without meaning. Appropriate pacing (knowing when to speed up and when to slow down) allows readers to interact with the text for better comprehension. Rayner (1998) explained this skill: "There are well-known individual differences in eye movement measures as a function of reading skill: Fast readers make shorter fixations, longer saccades, the jump of the eye from one fixation to another, and fewer regressions than slow readers" (p. 392).

Assisted reading provides the reader with support, good models of fluent readers, and helps to build fluency. The National Institute of Child Health and Human Development (National Reading Panel, 2000) asserted, "Classroom practices that encourage repeated oral reading with feedback and guidance lead to meaningful improvements in reading expertise for students—for good readers, as well as those who are experiencing difficulties" (p. 3). Assisted repeated reading can potentially develop weak world language readers' fluency and help them to become independent readers through a distinct form of scaffolding (Taguchi et al., 2004). Based on accumulated research evidence, second language researchers have found that this strategy is a promising method to develop second language readers' fluency and thereby improve their comprehension (Anderson, 1994).

Rereading or repeated reading is one of the most frequently recognized approaches to improving fluency (National Reading Panel, 2000; Rashotte & Torgesen, 1985). The technique of practicing something over and over again to improve performance is used by musicians and athletes. Repeated reading is a method created by Samuels (1979) in which readers reread a short passage silently or orally until the reader is able to read it with ease. Taguchi et al. (2004) determined that assisted repeated reading is equally as effective as extensive reading in increasing second language students' activities. With this strategy, world language learners read specified passages from text readings repeatedly in order to increase the readers' sign recognition of words and phrases, thereby increasing their reading fluency and comprehension (Blum et al., 1995; Taguchi & Gorsuch, 2002). Repeated reading has many benefits, including increasing students' oral reading rates and accuracy (Young, Bowers, & MacKinnon, 1996) and having positive effects on readers' vocabulary development (Koskinen & Blum, 1984); the practice effects also carry over to new, unpracticed passages with regard to reading rate and accuracy (Faulkner & Levy, 1994). One important note: for the carryover to new passages to be seen, there needs to be a degree of overlapping vocabulary between the old and new passages (Rashotte & Torgesen, 1985).

Comprehension Instruction

Comprehension is the essence of reading (Ruddell, Ruddell, & Singer, 1994). When it comes to reading, comprehension is the most important thing. The purpose for reading is for understanding. Readers are not only expected to think about what they are reading but also about what they are learning.

Educators now realize the complexity involved in reading for comprehension. Fielding and Pearson (1994) explained that reading used to be thought of as a natural result of decoding plus oral and language, but now comprehension is viewed as a complex process involving knowledge, experience, thinking, and teaching. While reading comprehension does involve a reader's literal understanding of the text, true reading comprehension goes beyond the superficial understanding of the text to the reader's interaction in constructing meaning from the text.

According to the National Reading Panel (2000), "Comprehension strategies are specific procedures that guide students to become aware of how well they are comprehending as they attempt to read and write" (pp. 4–5). Comprehension strategies include determining importance, questioning, predicting, interpreting, visualizing, inferring, drawing conclusions, summarizing, and informing (Dole, Duffy, Roehler, & Pearson, 1991; Long, Winograd, & Bridge, 1989). It is critical to teach students to think when they read so that they can access information to learn, remember, think about, and critique what they read.

Currently, there is no one right way to teach comprehension. The goal is not to teach strategies just for the sake of teaching comprehension strategies. The goal is to teach strategies so that students can use them to engage in reading and understand what they read. Comprehension strategies are only tools that readers use to construct meaning from text (Block & Pressley, 2002). Quality comprehension strategies help students to monitor their understanding, enhance their understanding, acquire and actively use knowledge, and develop insights into the reading.

Taught as a strategic process, comprehension allows students to move beyond simple literal recall to make connections and generate knowledge. Ellery (2005) asserted, "Teachers need to remember that good comprehension instruction needs to be taught explicitly and strategically" (p. 141). There is substantial research evidence that demonstrates that explicit comprehension instruction improves students' understanding (Block & Pressley, 2002; Block, Gambrell, & Pressley, 2002; National Reading Panel, 2000; Ruddell & Unrau, 2004). Routeman (2003) explained that teachers must "make the strategy a part of our unconscious reading process, so that students are able to combine any number of strategies to problem solve before, during, and after they read" (p. 129).

Much of the teaching responsibility when it comes to teaching reading is to make what is implicit, explicit. Teachers need to explain reading strategies so that readers can access and use them to construct meaning in their own reading. Pearson and Gallagher (1983) introduced a framework for instruction called the "Gradual Release of Responsibility." Using this framework, teachers teach a strategy by first modeling it for the students as a large class and then guiding students to practice that strategy in groups or pairs several times. Later, the teacher provides students with significant blocks of time for students to read independently and practice using and applying the reading strategies. Students need to be able to apply comprehension strategies flexibly and independently to become proficient readers.

Researchers in reading comprehension identified and systematically investigated strategies that proficient readers used when constructing meaning from text. Pearson, Dole, Duffy, and Roehler (1992) summarized these findings in the following list. Proficient readers do the following:

- Search for connections between what they know and new information they find in texts
- Ask questions of themselves and the texts they read
- Draw inferences during and after reading
- Distinguish between important and less important information in texts
- Adeptly synthesize information within and across texts and experience
- Monitor their comprehension and fix faulty comprehension

Keene and Zimmermann (1997) added imaging to this list of comprehension strategies. They found that proficient readers also visualize and create images using different senses to understand what they read.

Comprehension is the key to becoming a proficient reader. Effective comprehension instruction engages students in the text and takes students beyond the literal meaning of text to interaction with the text. To be effective, comprehension strategies require explicit and purposeful teaching on the part of the teacher.

Organization of This Book

Having shared some of the reading research and findings currently available in the first part of this book, the rest of this book is devoted to presenting information in a resource format so that teachers can better equip themselves in the craft of teaching L2 reading. Because no two teaching styles are exactly alike, various classrooms have different individual goals for reading, and the makeup of the students in these classrooms are different, we have organized the remainder of the book so teachers can easily select and utilize a variety of strategies and activities that address their need during pre-reading, during-reading, and post-reading.

The next section begins by identifying various **reading strategies**. Each strategy is presented by identifying the title of the strategy, a suggestion of when to use the strategy, and a description of the strategy. Then, the teacher will find an explanation of the purposes or goals for using the strategy. Next, a description is given on how to teach the students to use each strategy. Finally, suggestions are given for ways to adapt each strategy, when appropriate. Ideally, the procedure for each strategy should begin with the teacher modeling the entire strategy, followed by ample time for students to work towards independent use of the strategy. Teachers will want to select strategies that fit their particular reading purpose, their teaching style, and the needs of their individual students. Remember, the ultimate goal for strategically presenting reading strategies is for students to eventually become independent users of the strategies and to have such available at their disposal as L2 learners.

After the strategy section of the book, the next section identifies various **reading activities** that teachers can implement into their L2 classroom. Each activity is presented by identifying the title of the activity, a suggestion of when to use the activity, and a description of the activity. Then, the teacher will see an explanation of the purposes or goals for using the strategy. Next, the teacher will read about ideas on how to use the activity in the L2 classroom, along with a section on how to adapt the activity, if appropriate.

The idea behind the activity section of this book is for teachers to discover different ways to practice and present reading in the L2 classroom beyond simply using classroom time to translate sentences into English and complete comprehension questions at the end of a specific section or chapter. There are a variety of activities presented to help teachers expand their current reading activity repertoires by allowing teachers to select activities that practice and extend their current use of reading activities in their classrooms.

The final section of this book introduces Reader's Theater in the L2 classroom. If you have never tried using this concept, it is a great way to have L2 students build strong reading and comprehension skills in an interesting read-aloud format. This section begins by briefly explaining what Reader's Theater is and sharing the benefits of using Reader's Theater. Next, various ways to implement Reader's Theater into an L2 classroom are discussed along with ways to add interest to this technique. Finally, ideas are shared on how teachers might choose to differentiate instruction using Reader's Theater.

It is the authors' sincere hope that this book will serve as an easy, useful resource in helping you to implement reading research findings in effective, interesting ways within your L2 classroom that meet your students' needs and your own individual teaching style.

3 Reading Strategies

Reading Strategy Use Chart

Strategy Number	Name of Strategy	Before Reading	During Reading	After Reading
1	Annolighting the Text		X	X
2	Annotating the Text	X	X	X
3	Anticipation Guide	X		X
4	Background Knowledge Post-It Notes	X		
5	Bloom's Taxonomy Questions		X	X
6	Choral Reading		X	
7	Cognate, False Cognate, and False Friend Vocabulary		X	
8	Collaborative Annotation	X	X	X
9	"Five W's and an H"		X	X
10	Fluency Development Lesson (FDL)		X	
11	Gist Writing and Illustrations	X	X	
12	Graphic Organizers	X	X	X
13	Inferences from Visuals and Text	X	X	
14	Inferring the Meaning of Vocabulary from Text		X	
15	KWL Chart	X		X
16	Paired Reading		X	
17	Paired Summary			X
18	Picture Details		X	
19	Predict-O-Gram	X		
20	Predicting ABCs	X		
21	Rapid Retrieval of Information (RRI)	X	X	
22	Reciprocal Teaching		X	X
23	Say, Mean, Matter		X	

(continued)

Strategy Number	Name of Strategy	Before Reading	During Reading	After Reading
24	Semantic Comparison		X	X
25	SQ3R (Survey, Question, Read, Recite, Review)	X	X	X
26	Story Mapping			X
27	Summarizing		X	X
28	Textbook Activity Guide (TAG)		X	
29	Think Aloud		X	
30	Think-Pair-Share	X	X	X
31	Three-Column IQR Sheet		X	
32	Three-Two-One (3-2-1)		X	X
33	Three-Minute Pause		X	
34	Vocabulary Builder	X	X	X
35	Vocabulary Prediction Chart	X	X	X
36	Vocabulary Question Organizer		X	
37	Wordstorming	X		

Strategy 1:
Annolighting the Text

Title of Strategy: Annolighting the Text

When to Use the Strategy:

- During reading
- Post-reading

Description of Strategy: This strategy has students interact with the text by teaching students how to highlight effectively and how to make annotations about the text. Students highlight key words and phrases in a text and then annotate those highlights with notes in a specially designed column in the margin.

Purposes/Goals of Strategy:

- Identify main ideas, key concepts, and important details in a reading
- Reduce needed information efficiency from a text
- Improve reading proficiency
- Provide a means for students to review text in a concise manner
- Strengthen students' reading comprehension

Teaching Students to Use the Strategy:

1. Have students read the text once to get a clear idea of the focus of the entire text.
2. Divide the text into manageable chunks and on the second time through the text, have students highlight the text.
3. To highlight text effectively, teach students to eliminate every unnecessary word. The remaining highlighted text should allow the reader to still make sense out of the highlighted words when s/he rereads them. However, students should not be highlighting entire sentences.
4. It is possible to have students use different colored highlighters to represent different things: one color for main ideas, one color for different characters, one color for supporting details, and one color for things students have questions about.
5. You may want to teach this skill in a large group as guided practice first, before allowing students to work on the skill by themselves. Students do not naturally know what or how to highlight material effectively.

Example:

Reader's Text with Highlights	Annotations
At this point they came in sight of thirty or forty windmills that are on that plain. "Fortune," said Don Quixote to his squire, as soon as he had seen them, "is arranging matters for us better than we could have hoped. Look there, friend Sancho Panza, where thirty or more monstrous giants rise up, all of whom I mean to engage in battle and slay, and with whose spoils we shall begin to make our fortunes. For this is righteous warfare, and it is God's good service to sweep so evil a breed from off the face of the earth." "What giants?" said Sancho Panza. "Those you see there," answered his master, "with the long arms, and some have them nearly two leagues long." "Look, your worship," said Sancho. "What we see there are not giants but windmills, and what seem to be their arms are the vanes that turned by the wind make the millstone go." "It is easy to see," replied Don Quixote, "that you are not used to this business of adventures. Those are giants, and if you are afraid, away with you out of here and betake yourself to prayer, while I engage them in fierce and unequal combat." So saying, he gave the spur to his steed Rocinante, heedless of the cries his squire Sancho sent after him, warning him that most certainly they were windmills and not giants he was going to attack. He, however, was so positive they were giants that he neither heard the cries of Sancho, nor perceived, near as he was, what they were. "Fly not, cowards and vile beings," he shouted, "for a single knight attacks you." A slight breeze at this moment sprang up, and the great vanes began to move. "Though ye flourish more arms than the giant Briareus, ye have to reckon with me!" exclaimed Don Quixote, when he saw this. So saying, he commended himself with all his heart to his lady Dulcinea, imploring her to support him in such a peril. With lance braced and covered by his shield, he charged at Rocinante's fullest gallop and attacked the first mill that stood in front of him. But as he drove his lance-point into the sail, the wind whirled it around with such force that it shivered the lance to pieces. It swept away with it horse and rider, and they were sent rolling over the plain, in sad condition indeed.	*Don Quixote's Viewpoint* ● Fortune ● Thirty or more monstrous giants ● Engage in battle and slay giants ● From spoils we shall make our fortunes ● God's good service ● Long arms two leagues long ● Easy to see ● Fierce and unequal combat ● Single knight attacks *Sancho Panza's Viewpoint* ● What giants? ● Sancho sees windmills ● Arms are vanes *Action* ● Sancho cries they are windmills ● Don Quixote spurs steed towards windmills heedless of Sancho's cries ● Windmill vanes begin to move ● Don Quixote implores Dulcinea to support him ● Don Quixote braces lance and charges full speed ● Don Quixote drive lance-point into windmill sail *Results* ● Shivered lance to pieces ● Swept away horse and Don Quixote ● Sad condition *New Vocabulary* ● "leagues"—several miles ● "Briareus"—a hundred-armed giant from Greek mythology

Figure 3.1 Original text with highlights and summary

Adapting this Strategy:

1. Have students work in teams to effectively highlight the text with the minimum number of words possible, the end goal being that worthwhile information can be gleaned from the fewest words. The teacher may want to make this a contest between different groups of people.

Strategy 2:
Annotating the Text

Title of Strategy: Annotating the Text

When to Use the Strategy:

- Pre-reading
- During reading
- Post-reading

Description of Strategy: This strategy promotes active engagement with the text and promotes critical reading skills. It is an active reading strategy that improves student comprehension and helps students to learn and remember the text content using the student's own words. Annotation is creating a summation of the text or article by writing brief key points about the reading passage.

Purposes/Goals of Strategy:

- Provide a purpose for reading
- Help students construct meaning from text
- Improve student comprehension of the text passage
- Increase student concentration and attention to reading
- Create a study tool for students
- Offer an immediate formative assessment of student understanding

Teaching Students to Use the Strategy:

1. Decide which of the three objectives you wish to meet through annotating a particular piece: a) to identify the author's most important points, b) to recognize how the author's points fit together, or c) to note the reader's responses to the author's writing.
2. Teach the student a "notation system."
3. Or, create your own "notation system" that works for you and for your students. Then, teach it to your students.

    Here's *one* notation system to consider:

a. **Double underline** the author's explanation of the main point(s) and put **M.P.** in the margin to denote "**main point(s).**"
b. **Single underline** each major new claim or problem the author presents and write "claim 1," "claim 2," or "problem 1," "problem 2," and so on in the margin.

c. **Asterisk** (*) pieces of evidence like statistics or arguments and note in the margin the kind of evidence or information and its purpose.

d. Write "**conclusion**" in the margin at the point or points where the author draws conclusions.

e. Put a **question mark** (?) next to any points or parts of the text that are unclear to you as the reader.

f. Put an **exclamation mark** (!) next to passages to which you react strongly in agreement, disagreement, or interest.

g. Attach a **post-it note** next to parts of the text and write a brief reaction to the text as you read.

Here's *another* notation system to consider:

a. Have the student read the entire text **twice**. The *first time* have students read to get an idea about what the text is about in a general sense. The *second time* have the students mark concepts, vocabulary, examples, and definitions that the student feels are inconsistent, interesting, or important.

b. Have the student sum up each paragraph of important ideas in the student's own words in the margins of the text.

c. Have students note **C&E** ("cause & effect") and **C&C** ("comparison & contrast") in the margins of the text.

d. Note any passages the student doesn't understand with a **question mark** (?).

e. Have the students write questions they have in the margins, either to ask the teacher or to investigate later.

f. Students circle any confusing or unknown words or phrases to either ask the teacher or to look up later.

g. Write an **exclamation mark** (!) beside any passages that generate a strong positive or negative response. Then, have students write their responses in the margin of the text.

h. Mark **potential test questions** with the abbreviation **PTQ**.

Adapting this Strategy:

1. Have students complete this activity individually or with a partner to prepare for a class discussion or a writing prompt.

2. The teacher could differentiate what passage and/or technique different student groups will use to annotate the text.

3. The teacher could divide students into heterogeneous and homogeneous groups and could work with a specific group to annotate a passage while other groups work independently or in groups without the teacher's assistance.

Strategy 3:
Anticipation Guide

Title of Strategy: Anticipation Guide

When to Use the Strategy:

- Pre-reading
- Post-reading

Description of Strategy: An anticipation guide is a pre-reading activity that uses a set of questions to activate students' prior knowledge. The activity allows students a chance to make personal connections to the reading and to preview what the reading is about.

Purposes/Goals of Strategy:

- Identify main ideas, key concepts, and important details in a reading
- Encourage students to make personal connections with a reading
- Make predictions about a reading selection
- Strengthen students' reading comprehension

Teaching Students to Use the Strategy:

1. Identify the major concepts or themes covered in the pages that students will read.
2. Write a series of statements, no more than five or six, related to the major pieces of information. Make sure that some statements are false but seem plausible. Copy the statements on a three-column transparency, in which the first column is titled "Before Reading," the second column is titled "Information," and the third column is titled "After Reading."
3. Ask students to respond with "agree" or "disagree" in the "Before Reading" column as you read aloud each statement. If students are unsure of an answer, they should be encouraged to make an educated guess.
4. Reread each statement aloud, asking students to share whether they agreed or disagreed with the statement. Ask them to explain why.
5. Have students read the selection. Then ask them to fill in the "After Reading" column of the chart with their responses.
6. Revisit the guide with the students to check their responses.

Adapting this Strategy:

1. Have students create their own true/false statements about a reading assigned for homework. As a bell ringer review of the reading selection the next day in class, students switch their charts with a partner and write whether they "agree" or "disagree" with the statements made regarding the reading.

Strategy 4:
Background Knowledge Post-It Notes

Title of Strategy: Background Knowledge Post-It Notes

When to Use the Strategy:

- Pre-reading

Description of Strategy: This activity will help students to activate and connect to background knowledge and help motivate interest in the content of the text to be read.

Purposes/Goals of Strategy:

- Activate background knowledge
- Motivate student interest in the upcoming reading

Teaching Students to Use the Strategy:

1. Students are given a brief overview of the upcoming reading or book. If a brief overview already exists on the back of the book or in a summary form, the teacher can use it. If it doesn't exist, the teacher can create one including things such as the country of origin, the cultural topic to be explored, and a brief teaser of what will happen in the book.
2. Individually, students record "what I think I know" about the country, culture, or topic on individual post-it notes. Students record one thought per post-it note.
3. After students fill out their post-it notes individually with their own background knowledge and information, they share their post-it notes with a partner.
4. After partners share post-it notes, students share their information with the large group and post their post-it notes on various pieces of chart paper, labeled "country," "cultural topic," and "general knowledge."

Adapting this Strategy:

1. This strategy could be done in small groups after the individual "think-and-write" time.
2. The students could write the information into their notebooks after the large group sharing and they could periodically add to their notes as the class reads the text.

Strategy 5:
Bloom's Taxonomy Questions

Title of Strategy: Bloom's Taxonomy Questions

When to Use the Strategy:

- During reading
- Post-reading

Description of Strategy: This strategy encourages students to pose or respond to questions about the text. Students can create or respond to different types and levels of questions to increase their understanding of the text.

Purposes/Goals of Strategy:

- Formulate questions at different levels of Bloom's taxonomy about the text
- Answer questions at different levels of Bloom's taxonomy about the text
- Strengthen students' reading comprehension
- Encourage students to make personal connections to the text
- Develop questions and answers that reflect the progression of thinking

Teaching Students to Use the Strategy:

1. Teachers or students create questions about what they have read. By using Bloom's taxonomy format, teachers can direct students to go beyond simple answering of factual questions to a more diverse purpose for reading. This technique also helps students to progress their thinking and responding from a literal level to a deeper level. (**NOTE:** Not all levels need to be developed for every text selection. Using some type of variety will lead students to a greater purpose of reading.)
2. Students can work individually, in pairs, or in small groups to ask a variety of questions about the text.
3. After the questions are created, students exchange papers and attempt to answer each other's questions.
4. Papers are then returned to the original student(s) for correction and feedback.

Example: "Cinderella"

"Knowledge"—the recall of specific information	Questions About the Text	Answers to Questions
	Who was Cinderella?	
	With whom did she live?	
"Comprehension"—an understand of what was read	What was the main idea of the story?	
	Why didn't Cinderella's stepmother like her?	
"Application"—the converting of abstract content to concrete situations	How were the mice in the story like real people?	
	Cinderella was in disguise when she met the prince and, as a result, he wouldn't have recognized her outside of her disguise. Why, then, do you think Cinderella felt it was so important for her to go to the ball to meet the prince?	
"Analysis"—the comparison and contrast of the content to personal experiences	How would you have reacted as Cinderella's parent if you had found out she had defied you and left the house without your permission to go to the ball?	
	How does Cinderella compare to one of your friends?	
"Synthesis"—the organization of thoughts, ideas, and information from the content	Can you list the events of the story in sequence?	
	Do you know of any other stories about children having difficult childhoods that end up living "happily ever after" as adults?	
"Evaluation"—the judgment and evaluation of characters, actions, and outcome for personal reflection and understanding	Would you have defied your parents and family and gone in disguise to the ball? Why or why not?	
	Why do you think that the story of Cinderella has been told to children for many, many years?	

Figure 3.2 Sample question guide: Cinderella

Strategy 6:
Choral Reading

Title of Strategy: Choral Reading

When to Use the Strategy:

- During reading

Description of Strategy: In this strategy, groups of students verbally read aloud a specific text or portion of a specific text.

Purposes/Goals of Strategy:

- Build teamwork during reading
- Promote growth in sight reading and pronunciation of words
- Support from entire group to assist reticent readers
- Aid in the reader's fluency
- Allow students to practice rereading sections of text

Teaching Students to Use the Strategy:

1. The teacher selects a text to be read aloud by the group in union. Decide and mark which groups of students will be reading which portion of the text aloud. (This could be done by assigning character dialogues, specific refrains, or certain text pieces.)
2. The teacher makes the text accessible to each member of the group using individual books, an overhead projector, or chart paper.
3. Brainstorm with the students how they might use their voices to express meaning and to make the choral reading performance interesting through typographical signals, voice inflections, enthusiasm, and appropriate pacing.
4. Students practice reading the text chorally several times to perform the reading.

Adapting this Strategy:

1. Pairs or very small groups of students can each be given a line of the text, rather than a section of the text, to read in unison.
2. The teacher could divide the entire class in half and have each group read its assigned text alternately, in a back-and-forth performance.
3. Some of the text could be read individually by strong readers with only refrains or some specific passages being read chorally.

Strategy 7:
Cognate, False Cognate, and False Friend Vocabulary

Title of Strategy: Cognate, False Cognate, and False Friend Vocabulary

When to Use the Strategy:

- During reading

Description of Strategy: When students read in L2, they need to be able to identify cognate, false cognate, and false friend vocabulary to increase their understanding of a narrative passage. False cognates are words in different languages that are similar in form and meaning but have different roots. They appear to have a common linguistic origin (regardless of meaning) but actually do not. False friends are pairs of words in two languages that look and/or sound similar but differ in meaning. The two terms, "false cognates" and "false friends," are sometimes used incorrectly or interchangeably by some teachers who believe they are the same thing when, in fact, they are not.

Purposes/Goals of Strategy:

- Identify cognates, which are words that have similar pronunciations and spelling in both languages and frequently have the same meaning.
- Recognize false cognates, which are pairs of words in different languages that are similar in form and meaning but have different roots.
- Discriminate between cognates, false cognates, and false friends. False friends bear two distinct (and sometimes even opposite) meanings. However, a pair of false friends can sometimes be true cognates.

Teaching Students to Use the Strategy:

1. The teacher identifies a portion of the text or chapter for students that contain some type of combination of cognates, false cognates, and false friends.
2. Using graphic organizer lists, students work in pairs on a selected portion of text to identify the cognates, false cognates, and false friends in the target language and in English.
3. The teacher then leads a large group discussion for students to check their work.

Adapting this Strategy:

1. It is sometimes helpful to teach a lesson on these concepts outside of the text first. The teacher can google examples in business where words or phrases were used incorrectly by businesses in the target language.
2. The teacher can show the students the examples from business and have them try to discover what is wrong with the wording/meaning.

For example in Spanish:

*   When General Motors introduced the Chevy Nova in South America, it was apparently unaware that "no va" means "it won't go." After the company figured out why it wasn't selling any cars, it renamed the car in its Spanish markets to the Caribe.
*   Parker Pens translated the slogan for its ink, "Avoid Embarrassment—Use Quink," into Spanish as "Evite Embarazos—Use Quink"—which also means "Avoid Pregnancy—Use Quink."
*   An American T-shirt maker in Miami printed shirts for the Spanish market that promoted a visit by Pope John Paul II. Instead of "I saw the Pope (el Papa)," the shirts read, "I saw the potato (la papa)."

Strategy 8:
Collaborative Annotation

Title of Strategy: Collaborative Annotation

When to Use the Strategy:

- Pre-reading
- During reading
- Post-reading

Description of Strategy: This strategy is used after students have already completed their own individual annotations about a text passage. It is an effective way to expand on the original reader's annotations and thoughts, and this strategy can then lead to effective small or large group discussions about the text.

Purposes/Goals of Strategy:

- Process information about text passage
- Strengthen students' reading comprehension and understanding of text
- Identify main ideas, key concepts, and important details in a reading
- Encourage students to read critically

Teaching Students to Use the Strategy:

1. Teach students to annotate text using a class-wide "annotation system" so that students are using the same symbols and techniques to process the text.
2. After students have completed their individual annotations, put students in groups of three, four, or five students.
3. At a specified signal from the teacher, students pass their annotated writing of the text to their right. Each individual makes additional comments to the reader's annotations. This can be in the form of agreement, expansion on the reader's original thoughts, or asking/answering questions. (It is important that the students understand that their focus is to expand on the original reader's ideas and/or questions and not to simply add the ideas they wrote in their original annotated paper.)
4. Students need to sign their written annotated comments under the reader's original remarks.
5. Rotation continues at the teacher's signal until everyone at the table has had a chance to respond in writing to everyone's annotated paper in their small group. In this way, each student has had three or four people build and expand on his/her original ideas.

Adapting this Strategy:

1. Each student can be given different colored pens so the teacher can easily assess who has written what, along with the signatures.
2. You could give each student at the table different things to look for in the writing. For example: student one at each table could ask the original writer questions about his/her annotation, student two could check for identification of main ideas, student three could translate noted unfamiliar words and phrases for the original student, and student four could illustrate with a small picture what happens in each paragraph.

Strategy 9: "Five W's and an H"

Title of Strategy: "Five W's and an H"

When to Use the Strategy:

- During reading
- Post-reading

Description of Strategy: This strategy encourages students to pose or respond to questions about the text. Students can create or respond to different types and levels of questions to increase their understanding of the text.

Purposes/Goals of Strategy:

- Formulate questions about text
- Answer questions about text
- Strengthen students' reading comprehension
- Identify main ideas, key concepts, and important details in a reading
- Encourage students to read critically

Teaching Students to Use the Strategy:

1. Using basic journalism inquiry, create six types of questions from a designated section of text ("who, what, where, when, why, and how").
2. There are two ways to conduct this strategy:
   a. Either these questions can be pre-written by the teacher for students to answer individually or in pairs;
   b. Or the students can create the questions and then exchange papers and answer other students' questions in pairs or small groups.
3. Papers are then returned either to the teacher or to the student creators of the questions for correction and feedback.

Example:

"Who"	Questions About the Text	Answers to Questions
"What"		
"Where"		
"When"		
"Why"		
"How"		

Figure 3.3

Adapting this Strategy:

1. This strategy could be done as a "think-pair-share" activity or as a small group activity to create and answer questions.
2. Students could create a "newspaper article" or a "newspaper review" about the text.

Strategy 10:
Fluency Development Lesson (FDL)

Title of Strategy: Fluency Development Lesson (FDL)

When to Use the Strategy:

- During reading

Description of Strategy: A Fluency Development Lesson is a combination of "read-aloud," "choral reading," "listening to children read," and reading performance. This strategy is implemented over an extended period (Rasinski, Padak, Linek, & Sturtevant, 1994). This strategy is used with short texts or parts of texts of around 100–200 words and is used at least four times weekly. During the lesson, students listen to the teacher read the text to the class. Then, students read the text chorally, pair up and practice reading the text with a partner, and perform parts of the text for the whole class.

Purposes/Goals of Strategy:

- Promote meaningful reading
- Help students with word recognition
- Increase students' fluency levels

Teaching Students to Use the Strategy:

1. The teacher identifies the text to be used with this strategy.
2. Distribute one copy of the text to each student in the class.
3. Read the text to the students several times while the students listen and follow along silently, looking at their own copy of the text.
4. Start a discussion with the students about the meaning of the text reading.
5. Discuss with the students how reading with expression can enhance the meaning of the text and how it increases a reader's interest in listening to the verbal text.
6. With the teacher, have the class chorally read the text several times.
7. Divide all students in the class into pairs. Each partner in the pair practices reading the text a minimum of three times.
8. The listener gives positive feedback to the student about what he or she did well during the practice reading.

9. Then, invite pairs of student volunteers to perform their text for the large class.

10. As a wrap-up, ask students to individually identify several words from the text that they want to include in their individual word bank notes.

Adapting this Strategy:

1. For longer text pieces, students can be divided into groups of three or four with different students presenting different text portions or becoming actual characters in the script, if there is character dialogue in the text.

Strategy 11:
Gist Writing and Illustrations

Title of Strategy: Gist Writing and Illustrations

When to Use the Strategy:

- Pre-reading
- During reading

Description of Strategy: Students need to learn how to read for general information in the target language and not get caught up on stumbling over every unfamiliar word. This strategy helps students to use skimming and scanning techniques.

Purposes/Goals of Strategy:

- Skim for reading structures
- Scan for main points
- Read over unfamiliar words and phrases

Teaching Students to Use the Strategy:

1. Students fold a piece of paper into quarters, numbering the squares 1, 2, 3, and 4.
2. The teacher gives a certain amount of time for students to read a certain portion of the text.
3. After students read the passage, they write a one- or two-sentence summary in the target language about what the passage was about in Box 1. Then, students discuss their answers with another classmate in a "pair-share" format.
4. Next, students read the subsequent portion of the text. They bullet two or three main points of the passage individually in the target language in Box 2, and then share with a partner.
5. Then, the students read another portion of the text and illustrate what occurred in Box 3. Students share their illustrations in a pair-share format.
6. Finally, students make predictions about what will happen next in the text in Box 4.

Adapting this Strategy:

1. This strategy could be done in small groups after the teacher models what to do. Each group could do the activity on a large piece of chart paper and then share responses with the large group.

Strategy 12:
Graphic Organizers

Title of Strategy: Graphic Organizers

When to Use the Strategy:

- Pre-reading
- During reading
- Post-reading

Description of Strategy: A graphic organizer is a visual display showing relationships between facts, information, terms, or ideas. Graphic organizers come in many varieties and have been widely researched for their effectiveness in improving student learning. Studies by Hall and Strangman (2002) demonstrated that the use of graphic organizers improved students' comprehension and, to a greater extent, improved students' vocabulary knowledge. Other names for these organizers include knowledge maps, concept maps, story maps, cognitive organizers, concept diagrams, and advance organizers. Marzano, Pickering, and Pollock (2001) stated that graphic organizers are the "most common way to help students generate nonlinguistic representation" (p. 75).

Variety

Here are some of the types of graphic organizers a teacher may want to use:

- Cause-Effect Chart
- Classification Chart
- Concept Web
- Fishbone
- KWL Chart
- Matrix
- Mind Map
- Sequence/Flow Chart
- Spider Map
- SQ3R Chart
- Story Map
- T-Chart
- Thinking Tree
- Time Line Chart
- Two Story Map
- Venn Diagram

Purposes/Goals of Strategy:

- Address prior knowledge
- Develop background or essential learning
- Guide thinking
- Categorize or organize information
- Raise questions
- Predict solutions or conclusions
- Confirm or reject prior knowledge
- Connect new information to what has already been learned
- Outline or organize thoughts and learning

Teaching Students to Use the Strategy:

1. The teacher should conduct an internet search to find graphic organizers that fit with the type of reading that is being conducted. A Google search on graphic organizers will provide many choices. Alternatively, the teacher could use software packages like Kidspiration or Inspiration.
2. It is helpful for the teacher to model the use of the type of graphic organizer first with another text passage. The teacher should model what quality completion of the organizer looks like, along with modeling what s/he is metacognitively processing as s/he determines what to write within the graphic organizer.
3. As a next step, it is often helpful to do one together with student input before allowing students to fill them out themselves.

Adapting this Strategy:

1. Once students are comfortable with various graphic organizers, give students a text passage and ask them to select a graphic organizer they feel is appropriate for the text passage, fill it out, and then share why they selected a particular graphic organizer.
2. Instead of filling out graphic organizers individually, the strategy can be done in pairs or small groups.

Strategy 13:
Inferences from Visuals and Text

Title of Strategy: Inferences from Visuals and Text

When to Use the Strategy:

- Pre-reading
- During reading

Description of Strategy: This activity will help students to rely on both pictures and text to predict outcomes, infer ideas, and construct meaning from the text.

Purposes/Goals of Strategy:

- Generate and test hypotheses from visual and text clues
- Predict outcomes
- Make inferences

Teaching Students to Use the Strategy:

1. Divide the students into small groups and give each group a piece of chart paper.
2. Students divide a piece of chart paper into two columns with one labeled "Quote or Picture from Text" and the second labeled "Inference."
3. Students look at the pictures, headings, or illustrations and brainstorm what they believe will happen in a particular chapter or text reading.
4. Students write their ideas, using either visual or text quotes in the appropriate columns.
5. As the story is read aloud, the teacher stops and asks students questions, using cues from the text.
6. Students continue to write their ideas in the appropriate columns.
7. At the end of the chapter or reading, students put a "+" beside items that were confirmed in the reading and a "−" beside the items that were contradicted.

Adapting this Strategy:

1. This strategy could be done in pairs after the teacher models what to do. Each student could have an identical sheet and at a predetermined time limit or by a teacher signal, students could respond on paper, making predictions and hypotheses, and supporting their guesses by visual or text clues.
2. This could be done as an entirely listening activity. Students would be provided with a visual but no text. The teacher would read sections of the text aloud and periodically stop. Student would then make written predictions and hypotheses supporting their guesses by information they heard or visuals they saw during the read aloud.

Strategy 14:
Inferring the Meaning of Vocabulary from Text

Title of Strategy: Inferring the Meaning of Vocabulary from Text

When to Use the Strategy:

- During reading

Description of Strategy: This strategy teaches students to use context clues to discover the meaning of unfamiliar vocabulary words.

Purposes/Goals of Strategy:

- Have students use context clues in the text to decode vocabulary meaning
- Teach students a different strategy to understand unfamiliar vocabulary rather than standard dictionary use
- Use one of the quickest and most effective ways of dealing with unfamiliar vocabulary by inferential thinking

Teaching Students to Use the Strategy:

1. The students (or the teacher in advance) create a four-column think sheet for each of the students.
2. At the top of the sheet in each of the four columns, students write "Unfamiliar Vocabulary," "Inferred Meaning," "Clue," and "Sentence."
3. As a text is read aloud, students raise their hand to signal an unfamiliar vocabulary word.
4. Students write the vocabulary word or phrase in the first column labeled "Unfamiliar Vocabulary."
5. Next, students try to guess the meaning of the words. Ways in which students might do this include strategies such as reading on, rereading, and looking for context clues like visual pictures or related words.
6. Students then fill in the "Inferred Meaning" column with what they believe the word or phrase means.
7. Then, students fill in what they used to infer the meaning in the "Clue" column.
8. Finally, the students create a new sentence that incorporates the unfamiliar target word or phrase in the final column labeled "Sentence."

Adapting this Strategy:

1. This strategy could be done in small groups while the teacher circulates from group to group, monitoring their progress. Charts could then be debriefed in the full classroom setting at a designated time for students to share what words each group found as unfamiliar and how they inferred the meaning of the vocabulary word or phrase.

2. One student in the class or small group could be designated to look up the word in the dictionary to confirm or deny the inferred meaning of the unfamiliar target word or phrase.

Strategy 15: KWL Chart

Title of Strategy: KWL Chart

When to Use the Strategy:

- Pre-reading ("K" and "W" columns)
- Post-reading ("L" column)

Description of Strategy: This strategy activates prior knowledge and guides students through a text. This is a group instruction activity. This strategy works best with expository texts.

Purposes/Goals of Strategy:

- Elicit students' prior knowledge of the information in the text
- Identify a purpose for reading
- Focus students' attention on their comprehension
- Provide an opportunity for students to expand ideas outside of the text

Teaching Students to Use the Strategy:

1. The teacher develops a three-column poster, KWL (Ogle, 1986), with each question in a column and elicits student responses to these questions: What do I **K**now? What do I **W**ant to learn? What did I **L**earn?
2. The teacher engages groups of students or leads a large classroom discussion to guide the readers and to fill in the KWL chart. This strategy serves as a model for active thinking during reading.

What do I **K**now?	What do I **W**ant to Know?	What did I **L**earn?

Figure 3.4 KWL chart

The "**K**" (**K**now) category is an advance organizer that provides the student with a background to the new material and acts as a pre-reading inventory. In leading a classroom discussion of this column, it is important to record all thoughts until the class cannot think of any more. It may be helpful to organize these thoughts into general categories if your class generates a lengthy list.

The "**W**" (**W**ant) category lists a series about what you want to know more of regarding the subject based on what was written in the "**K**" column. Eliciting information about the "**W**" column can be accomplished by previewing the table of contents, headings, pictures, etc. Students generate a list of what they want or expect to learn in the reading. Then, they turn all the sentences into questions and write them in the column. This serves to focus students' attention as they read.

The "**L**" (**L**earn) category is completed after the "**K**" and "**W**" columns are completed, after the whole reading (or as sections of the reading are completed). Students compare their information with the "**W**" column, where they listed what they wanted or expected to learn from the reading. Students can use symbols in this column next to statements. For example, "M" can be written next to "main ideas," "!" next to surprising pieces of information, and "?" next to things that students still have questions about or feel they don't understand fully.

Adapting this Strategy:

1. You may wish to add a fourth column, labeled "**H**," to the chart. The "**H**" (**H**ow) category stands for having students identify *how they can learn more*; students can locate or identify other sources where additional information on the topic could be found.

Strategy 16:
Paired Reading

Title of Strategy: Paired Reading

When to Use the Strategy:

- During reading

Description of Strategy: Paired reading is a one-on-one tutorial in which a struggling reader is paired with a strong reader. The strong reader might be another classmate, an age-level peer, an older student, or an adult who will serve as a reading tutor. This strategy has been found to result in remarkable progress, accelerating the student's comprehension and word recognition when done regularly (Topping, 1987). The two sit side by side and read one self-selected text together, with either the student or the other person pointing to the text as it is read.

Purposes/Goals of Strategy:

- Provide a model for the student of how the reading should sound
- Allow the student to read on his/her own in a one-on-one setting
- Give support to a struggling student
- Accelerate reading comprehension
- Improve word recognition

Teaching Students to Use the Strategy:

1. The student chooses the reading material and is permitted to change it at any time, even during the reading.
2. The student and the tutor begin by reading together.
3. The student establishes a signal (e.g., a nod of the head) to indicate to the tutor that the student wants to read aloud solo.
4. As the student reads, the tutor supports the student as he or she reads aloud.
5. At logical times, the tutor and the student stop to talk about the meaning of what is being read.
6. If the student miscues, the tutor waits to see if the student self-corrects. If the student doesn't self-correct and the miscue alters the meaning, the tutor points to the word and asks, "what would this be?" If possible, the student supplies the word. If not, the tutor supplies the word.
7. The student and the tutor continue reading verbally together until the student signals to the tutor that he or she would like to read solo again.

Adapting this Strategy:

1. The student and the tutor could practice a self-selected text piece to do as a performance piece for the rest of the class. Some parts of the text passage could be read as a duo part and some could be read as a solo part at the discretion of the student and tutor.

Strategy 17:
Paired Summary

Title of Strategy: Paired Summary

When to Use the Strategy:

- Post-reading

Description of Strategy: First, students write a summary independently. Then, working with a partner, students elaborate on their retellings of a passage or story they have read.

Purposes/Goals of Strategy:

- Focus students' attention on the value of individual preparation and community participation
- Specify what each partner understood from the reading
- Identify what they collectively could not come to understand from the reading
- Formulate questions for their classmates and teacher

Teaching Students to Use the Strategy:

1. Students read a text passage or text selection individually.
2. Immediately after reading, each student writes an individual retelling of the text selection in the target language. If a student has difficulty remembering what happened, the student should refer to the text to verify or recue his/her thinking. However, as much as possible, students should strive to write the retelling without looking back at the text.
3. Students are assigned partners. When students have finished writing their individual retelling, the partners exchange papers. Partner A writes an abstract of partner B's retelling and vice versa. At this stage students are not allowed to converse with one another. If something is not clear to one of the partners, he or she must work to figure out what was intended.
4. When the abstracts are completed, the pair discusses the retellings and abstracts. During the discussion they do each of the following:
   - Specify what each understood as readers of the retellings
   - Identify what they collectively cannot understand in the story they read to create their individual retellings
   - Formulate questions for their classmates and teacher
5. When each pair of students has completed the tasks, the entire class discusses the questions prepared by the students and/or shares the abstracts they have written in the target language.

Adapting this Strategy:

1. If students are having difficulty writing a retelling individually, the teacher could have the partners go immediately from reading individually to discussing the text and writing an abstract together in the target language.
2. Students might want to compete with their partners to see who can write the most details about the text reading without referring to the text after it is read for the first time.

Strategy 18:
Picture Details

Title of Strategy: Picture Details

When to Use the Strategy:

- During reading

Description of Strategy: It is important when reading that students not only be taught how to read for big ideas but also for details. Careful reading of a text by paying attention to details is central to understanding the text.

Purposes/Goals of Strategy:

- Read for specific pieces of information and details
- Convey reading comprehension through a nonlinguistic representation

Teaching Students to Use the Strategy:

1. In order to teach students the importance of reading for details, the teacher picks a particularly interesting, detailed section of the text. Instead of having students respond in writing to the scene or translate what they have read, the students will draw what has happened in the scene, adding as many details from the text as possible.

Adapting this Strategy:

1. This strategy could be done in small groups or in student pairs so a discussion can occur about what is important to include in the illustration.
2. The teacher could reverse this activity by giving students a detailed picture and asking individual or pairs of students to write about the details in the picture in the target language.
3. The teacher could read a detailed section of the text aloud. (Students would not see a written copy of the script.) As the teacher reads the text, the students draw any and all details they hear in a picture.

Strategy 19:
Predict-O-Gram

Title of Strategy: Predict-O-Gram

When to Use the Strategy:

- Pre-reading

Description of Strategy: A Predict-O-Gram (Blachowicz, 1986) uses known and unknown words, phrases, places, and dates to predict story plots and character relationships. This strategy focuses students' discussion around a narrow selection of words as they predict how these words will be used in the upcoming text.

Teaching Students to Use the Strategy:

1. The teacher selects between 10 and 20 vocabulary words or phrases from an upcoming text reading and writes them on a piece of paper for each student, or on an overhead transparency. The teacher wants to balance the selection on this list with vocabulary words, phrases, places, and dates he or she knows the student will recognize with unfamiliar vocabulary words, phrases, places, and dates.
2. Have the students individually predict how they think the author will use these words to tell the story.
3. Once students have individually brainstormed responses, they should share their responses in pairs or small groups.
4. Then, volunteers share their predictions with the rest of the class.

Adapting this Strategy:

1. This strategy could be done immediately in small groups without the individual component.
2. Each group of students could be asked to make five predictions for the upcoming chapter. The teacher could hold a competition to see which student group makes the highest number of correct predictions out of five.

Strategy 20:
Predicting ABCs

Title of Strategy: Predicting ABCs

When to Use the Strategy:

- Pre-reading

Description of Strategy: Predicting ABCs is a pre-reading strategy in which students can anticipate words, names, or grammatical concepts they expect to find in a reading (Little, 2007).

Purposes/Goals of Strategy:

- Strengthen students' reading comprehension
- Reflect on unit objectives, and the lexical and grammatical concepts to achieve them
- Help students to remember more deeply the reading

Teaching Students to Use the Strategy:

1. Explain to students that a good reading strategy is to think about key words they might find in a text about a certain topic before they read it.
2. Provide students with a Predicting ABCs chart. The chart provides alphabetically labeled squares to prompt students' reactions.
3. Introduce the topic and/or title of the reading. You may also want to show them storyboards/pictures from the reading, if they are available. Ask students to think about what words and phrases they know that they would expect to find in the reading.
4. Give students time to record alphabetically applicable words and phrases.
5. Then, instruct them to skim the reading section, circling words and phrases on their chart that are actually included in the reading.
6. Ask students about the words and phrases they predicted that they also found in the text. Review the meanings and translations of the words and phrases.

Adapting this Strategy:

1. You could make a competition out of this strategy. Have students work in pairs to think of the most terms.

Sample chart:
Predicting ABCs

Skill: Previewing Vocabulary

A-B	C-D	E-F	G-I
J-K	L-LL	M-N	O-P
Q-R	S-T	U-W	X-Z

Figure 3.5 Blank ABC chart

Strategy 21:
Rapid Retrieval of Information (RRI)

Title of Strategy: Rapid Retrieval of Information (RRI)

When to Use the Strategy:

- Pre-reading
- During reading

Description of Strategy: Rapid Retrieval of Information (Green, 1998) is a strategy to use for previewing or reviewing material to help students locate specific information in the text passage. In this strategy, students orally reread information found in the text to provide an answer to a question or to help verify a specific point.

Purposes/Goals of Strategy:

- Locate specific information within a text passage
- Distinguish between relevant information and irrelevant information to answer or verify a point of view
- Find information quickly

Teaching Students to Use the Strategy:

1. The teacher gives the students a text to read.
2. Allow the students to read the text in class silently.
3. Once everyone has read the text silently, present a specific task for a student to do. Specific tasks might include: asking a student to read aloud a sentence about how a character feels or how a character was treated, find a phrase that defines a vocabulary word, identify information to support or prove a specific point, find a sentence that describes a specific point, read sentences that compare two items, or locate sentences that support one's point.
4. Ask students to listen to the task and reread (silently) appropriate parts of the text to address the task.
5. Once students have located the information, have them signal by raising their hand or holding up a signal card.
6. Once the teacher calls on the student, he or she reads aloud the information from the text.
7. The teacher continues to call on other students for a variety of responses.

Adapting this Strategy:

1. Text that can be used for this activity can be one page in length or longer, such as an entire chapter.
2. The teacher can use a variety of text types in the target language to have students practice: narrative, informational, persuasive, cultural, etc.

Strategy 22: Reciprocal Teaching

Title of Strategy: Reciprocal Teaching

When to Use the Strategy:

- During reading
- Post-reading

Description of Strategy: Reciprocal teaching is a strategy created by Palincsar and Brown (1986) that involves a dialogue between the teacher and students or students and other students regarding sections of a text. The dialogue consists of four strategies: summarizing, question generating, clarifying, and predicting. The teacher and students take turns assuming the role of teacher in leading this dialogue.

Purposes/Goals of Strategy:

- Facilitate a dialogue about sections of a text
- Provide a deeper understanding of a text
- Collaborate in understanding a selection of content

Teaching Students to Use the Strategy:

1. Students need to be taught and have this strategy modeled before they are allowed to use this strategy.
2. Put students in groups of four.
3. Distribute one index card to each member of the group identifying each person's unique role and a brief description of each role:
   - Summarizer
   - Questioner
   - Clarifier
   - Predictor
4. Have students read a few paragraphs of the assigned text selection. Encourage them to use note-taking strategies such as selective underlining or sticky notes to help them better prepare for their role in the discussion.
5. At the given stopping point, the **Summarizer** will highlight the key ideas up to this point in the reading.
6. The **Questioner** will then pose questions about the selection, regarding issues such as:
   - Unclear parts
   - Puzzling information

- Connections to other concepts already learned
- Motivations of the agents, actors, or characters

7. The **Clarifier** will address confusing parts and attempt to answer the questions that were just posed.

8. The **Predictor** can offer guesses about what the author will tell the group next or, if it's a literary selection, s/he might suggest what the next events in the story will be.

9. The roles in the group then switch one person to the right, and the next selection is read. Students repeat the process using their new roles. This continues until the entire selection is read.

Adapting this Strategy:

1. One approach to reciprocal teaching is to have students work from a four-column chart, with each column headed by the different comprehension activity involved, and to run the activity as a whole-class activity to teach students what to do when they are in small groups.

Strategy 23:
Say, Mean, Matter

Title of Strategy: Say, Mean, Matter

When to Use the Strategy:

- During reading

Description of Strategy: It is effective for all student levels from language learners to AP students. It can be used with academic texts, fiction, and non-verbal material. The strategy uses a three-column chart. This can be on an overhead, chart paper, chalkboard, or whatever is handy. Once students have learned the method, they can quickly draw the graphic organizer and use it to find meaning and significance. "Say," "Mean," and "Matter" are the three column titles on the chart.

Purposes/Goals of Strategy:

- Examine surface features and deeper meanings of both fiction and non-fiction texts
- Provide students with a starting point for a literary analysis essay

Teaching Students to Use the Strategy:

1. When initially teaching the strategy, explain what each column means, using age-appropriate directions and suggestions.
2. To first teach the strategy, you might use a short text or cartoon (single frame or strip) to demonstrate how text provides information on several levels.
3. First, elicit from the students what the text *says*, what words are actually used, or if a cartoon, what the drawing illustrates.
4. Students may also paraphrase the language. The text should be "right there." When filling in the chart, it may be helpful to number the responses.
5. For each item on the "Say" list, ask the students what they believe the statement *means*. As these are suggested, write them in the second column, discussing them along the way. Ask questions such as "what makes you think that?" and "how do you know that?"
6. The third column, "Matter," is the most abstract and may prove to be difficult at first. Ask: "so what?," "what is the theme of the piece?," "how does this piece connect to your own life?," "what does it matter to you?," "what questions does this piece raise?," or "what implications does it hold for a given group of people or for people in general?" In this column you find the meaning and depth of the piece.

SAY	MEAN	MATTER
What does the text say? What happened? Cite text (quotation) or paraphrase.	What does the author mean? How do I interpret this? Read "between the lines."	Why does it matter to me or others? Why is this important? What is the significance? What are the implications?

Figure 3.6 Three-column title chart

7. Once students learn how the three columns are used to understand a cartoon or short piece of text, a next step might be to have the class generate a paragraph to explain or analyze the piece. Use the ideas recorded on the chart to create the paragraph. One way to do this is to start with a statement from the "Matter" column as a topic or thesis statement, and then draw on the "Say" and "Mean" columns for supporting details. The first column provides "text proof" (what the text says), whereas the second column provides student interpretation. (Teacher should model initial steps of the writing; then students can complete it on their own, or with a partner.)

Adapting this Strategy:

1. When "Say, Mean, Matter" is applied to a longer text (a chapter in a textbook, a story, or even a novel), the columns can be used to help structure an essay, using the same process as when writing a paragraph.
2. Another writing approach is to conglomerate ideas according to a number of "mean" ideas and to support these with "say" items. The introduction and/or conclusion may come from a "matter" idea. The writer can start anywhere and build a coherent analysis of the text.
3. The strategy can also be used orally once students are familiar with it. The teacher can stop in the middle of a class reading and quickly do an oral run through of the three columns, asking "what is this saying?," "what does it mean?," and "why does it matter?" This encourages higher-level thinking during reading, and is especially useful when the text is complex.

Strategy 24:
Semantic Comparison

Title of Strategy: Semantic Comparison

When to Use the Strategy:

- During reading
- Post-reading

Description of Strategy: A semantic grid is a strategy for graphically representing important concepts and showing relationships in a reading. This strategy allows students deeper comprehension of a reading by elaborating and refining knowledge about a reading. A set of concepts are listed down the left side of a grid. Then, characters, criteria, or features are listed across the top of the grid.

Purposes/Goals of Strategy:

- Organize knowledge about reading into relationships
- Provide a graphic structure of knowledge for students to organize new ideas as they are understood

	Don Quixote	Sancho Panza
Realist	N	Y ("start" of novel) N ("end" of novel)
Idealist	Y	N ("start" of novel) Y ("end" of novel)
Wanted to do good deeds for no reward	Y	N
Wanted payment for work	N	Y
Lived with family members	Y	Y

Figure 3.7 Sample grid: Don Quixote

Teaching Students to Use the Strategy:

1. A set of concepts is listed down the left side of the chart.
2. At the top of the rows of the chart, a listing is made of characters, criteria, or features.
3. If the concept is associated with the character, criteria, or feature, the student records a "Y" ("Yes") in the grid where the column and row intersect.
4. If the concept is not associated with the character, criteria, or feature, the student records an "N" ("No") in the grid where the column and row intersect.

Adapting this Strategy:

1. The left column and the rows at the top of the grid could be previously filled in by the teacher through a large group discussion, or students could brainstorm the categories to write in the grid before marking "Y" or "N." Some portions of the grid could have both "Y" and "N" in the space if things transpired or changed throughout the book.
2. This strategy can be used to compare two different readings or two different books.

Strategy 25:
SQ3R (Survey, Question, Read, Recite, Review)

Title of Strategy: SQ3R (Survey, Question, Read, Recite, Review)

When to Use the Strategy:

- Pre-reading
- During reading
- Post-reading

Description of Strategy: SQ3R is an acronym that stands for a combination of various reading strategies that include:

- Survey (determine the structure or organization of the chapter)
- Question (turn each heading/subheading of a reading into a question)
- Read (read selectively)
- Recite (answer questions in your own words)
- Review (immediate and delayed review)

Purposes/Goals of Strategy:

- Establish a purpose for reading
- Help students to read with more efficiency
- Facilitate recall of the material read

Teaching Students to Use the Strategy:

1. Before students read a passage or a chapter, they survey the reading, which includes:
   - Guessing what the reading is about by considering the title
   - Reading the introduction to get a sense for what the reading will be about
   - Reading any headings in boldface; they will be main ideas of the reading
   - Reading any comprehension questions before reading the text, as they will give insight as to what the reading is about
2. Following the survey, students will have gained input that can be turned into questions. Questions that may come to mind might include those pertaining to character development, main events, and plot and setting. Students should write down their questions and answer them after reading.
3. Next, students read the assigned passage, looking for answers to their questions from step two.
4. In the recite stage, students write in their own words answers to their questions.

5. Finally, the teacher should provide immediate review and delayed review opportunities for students. An example of an immediate review would be the teacher directing the class to read a passage and then assigning a follow-up task to the reading, such as an oral recitation in the target language of what was read or a brief discussion of the passage in pairs. A delayed review could be a paired Q/A session the following day in class or a series of questions about the previous day's reading presented as a "bell ringer" at the beginning of the next class.

Adapting this Strategy:

1. The teacher could prepare, ahead of time, differentiated SQ3R guides that require students to complete the five steps of the strategy at varying complexity levels. For example, in the second step of the strategy, questioning, the teacher could require a student to come up with original questions on one version of the guide, whereas on another version the teacher could supply a list of word prompts to assist weaker readers with forming questions about the text.

Strategy 26:
Story Mapping

Title of Strategy: Story Mapping

When to Use the Strategy:

- Post-reading

Description of Strategy: This strategy instructs the reader about the interrelated parts of a story or selection and provides a framework that draws the reader's attention to the common elements of a story:

> **Setting:** Where and when did the event take place? Over what period of time?
>
> **Characters:** Who was involved?
>
> **Problem/Goal:** What sets the events of the story in motion? What problem arises? What goal were the characters after?
>
> **Key Episodes:** What were the key events that happened in the story?
>
> **Resolution/Outcome:** How was the problem solved? Was the goal reached?
>
> **Theme:** What was the personal or universal truth from the story?

Purposes/Goals of Strategy:

- Enhance students' interpretative abilities by enabling them to visualize story characters, events, and settings
- Increase students' comprehension of selections by organizing and sequencing main story events
- Serve as a framework for storytelling and retelling, and for story writing

Teaching Students to Use the Strategy:

1. Students read a passage or text.
2. Provide students with a handout of a story map of the passage or text.
3. On the story map, include an explanation of each story element and instructions that guide students to analyzing each element.
4. Students complete the instructions in each part of the story map.
5. Teacher and students discuss each section of the story map.

Adapting this Strategy:

1. [For struggling readers] Instead of a story map that features questions about each story element, students could choose from already supplied statements that

analyze each element. In other words, students would choose the statement that correctly describes the element, as though it were a multiple-choice test.

Information for the Teacher	Directions for the Student
Setting: Writers let the reader know where and when the story takes place.	Filling in the three pieces of information about the setting of the story. Information that shows WHEN this story happened: Information that shows WHERE this story took place: In WHAT PLACES did this story take place:
Characters: All stories have characters. They may be people, animals, or objects that the writer uses to tell the story.	Write the names of the characters found in the story and identify something the author has written about the character. Character's Name Tell something the author has written about this character 1. 2. 3.
Problem/Goal: Stories have action. The writer usually tells the reader about the characters and the problems they face with actions characters do to deal with their problems.	What was the first problem encountered in the book? How did the character(s) deal with the problem? Is there another problem encountered in the book? How did the character(s) deal with the problem?
Key Episodes: In a story, key events occur throughout the story.	List the key events that happen in the story. List them in the order that they happened from the beginning to the end of the reading. 1. 2. 3. 4. 5. 6. 7.
Resolution/Outcome: In a story, the reader needs to determine if the problem was resolved and/or if the character's goal was met.	Describe the resolution or outcome of the story:
Theme: This is the "so what?" of a story map. This is the personal truth or universal truth as in the larger meaning or importance.	Write a sentence or two about the conclusion explaining how things worked out for the characters:

Figure 3.8 Sample story map handout

Strategy 27:
Summarizing

Title of Strategy: Summarizing

When to Use the Strategy:

- During reading
- Post-reading

Description of Strategy: This strategy helps students to develop a brief synopsis of a larger section of text by focusing on the gist, key words, and main ideas found in a reading.

Purposes/Goals of Strategy:

- Help students to pull out main ideas
- Focus students on key details
- Break down larger ideas
- Encourage students to write succinct notes

Teaching Students to Use the Strategy:

1. For students to get this strategy, it has to be modeled many times by the teacher and practiced many times by the students in order to do it well.
2. Have students do selective underlining on a section of a reading. Tell students they are to focus on "who, what, when, where, why, and how" in their underlining.
3. Then, have the students turn over the paper and create a summary paragraph of the key ideas in the section.
4. Students should go back and forth, looking at their underlining and then writing the paragraph until they have it completed.
5. Then have students rewrite their piece, preserving the essential and relevant information but having a word limit (or, a number of words that they have to drop from their original writing).

Adapting this Strategy:

1. Give students a piece of paper that has lines for each word the student is going to write, and a maximum word limit. Students must summarize a reading section using a certain number of words.

Example: _____

_____

_____ [25 words]

2. Have students read a short section of the newspaper and then create a headline for the news story. Limit the number of words they can use.
3. Make it a contest to see which students can keep the essential information in a reading section summary while using the fewest words possible.

Strategy 28:
Textbook Activity Guide (TAG)

Title of Strategy: Textbook Activity Guide (TAG)

When to Use the Strategy:

● During reading

Description of Strategy: Textbook Activity Guide (TAG) (Johns & Lenski, 1997) is a paired strategy in which students have the opportunity to interact with the text in a variety of ways, and the teacher can design this activity to integrate strategies like predicting, reading and discussing, skimming, and reading and retelling. This strategy is easily adapted to any text, textbook, or content area of instruction, and easily customized to the skills the teacher wants the students to practice.

Purposes/Goals of Strategy:

● Improve students' comprehension
● Help students to organize information and to show relationships
● Help students to summarize and retell information
● Engage students in communication skills
● Allow students to self-monitor when the teacher provides a guide for the students
● Practice prediction skills

Teaching Students to Use the Strategy:

1. The teacher selects a text or identifies a chapter to use with this strategy.
2. Next, the teacher clarifies the lesson objective and matches the reading or study task to the objective.
3. The teacher then creates a study guide based on the lesson objectives.

   Here's an example of what a study guide might look like:

   Self-Monitoring Check

   Name: _____ **Class:** _____

   After completing the TAG strategy with my partner on this text selection:

   _____ I understand the information.

   _____ I'm not sure that I understand the information.

   _____ I do not understand the information and I need to restudy the information.

4. The teacher introduces the TAG study guide to the students and models the expectations for activity completion.

Adapting this Strategy:

1. The teacher can adapt this strategy to include any target strategies that meet the lesson's objectives and are strategies the teacher wants the students to practice.
2. This strategy is easily adapted to any type of text information, any length of text, and any content area of information.

PP	Predict with partner
RDP	Read information silently and discuss with partner
SKDP	Skim silently by reading quickly and discuss with partner
RR	Read information silently and retell with partner (verbally or written form)
WR	Write an individual response
WRDP	Write an individual response and discuss with partner
MCO	Make a map, chart, or outline of information

1. _____ PP	[Note the page numbers here.] Survey the title, pictures, and headings for this chapter. After you discuss ideas with your partner, write down what you think you will learn in this chapter.
2. _____ RDP	[Note page numbers here.] Do the first three paragraphs on these pages.
3. _____ SKDP	[Note page numbers here.] Skim these pages to define the author's purpose in telling the reader this information.
4. _____ RR	[Note the page numbers here.] Retell with your partner first verbally what you have learned in this section. Then, retell in writing what you have learned.
5. _____ WR	[Note the page numbers here.] As you are reading, jot down key words in this section and write down definitions if you know what these words mean.
6. _____ WRDP	[Note the page numbers here.] Read these first four paragraphs and write a short summary on the main ideas found in this selection.
7. _____ MCO	Map: [Note the page number here]. Draw a map as a visual representation of the information on this page.

Figure 3.9 Sample TAG chart

Strategy 29: Think Aloud

Title of Strategy: Think Aloud

When to Use the Strategy:

- During reading

Description of Strategy: During the "Think Aloud" strategy, the teacher verbalizes his or her thoughts so students can see what good readers do to enhance comprehension. In particular, Davey (1983) identified five strategies that poor readers often lack: predicting, forming mental images while reading, accessing prior knowledge about the topic, monitoring comprehension through clarification or summarization, and fixing problems while reading. The teacher can highlight these strategies through the "think aloud" strategy by modeling a few at a time in various "think alouds."

Purposes/Goals of Strategy:

- Visualize strategies good readers use to help them comprehend text
- Show students how to make predictions
- Encourage students to form mental images
- Demonstrate how to access prior knowledge
- Provide a model to help students to monitor comprehension

Teaching Students to Use the Strategy:

1. The teacher selects a passage to read aloud. (This passage should have some difficulty to appropriately model the use of various comprehension strategies like ambiguous text or unfamiliar words.)
2. The teacher begins reading the text aloud and students follow along.
3. As the teacher reaches a difficult part of the text, s/he should stop and think the text part through so that students can hear how information is processed. (You might choose a predicting strategy, show how to form a mental image, access prior knowledge, monitor comprehension, or use another strategy to work through that portion of the text.)
4. Ask the students to add their thoughts and suggestions to yours in helping to process and to comprehend the text.

Adapting this Strategy:

1. After you have modeled a "think aloud" strategy several times, have the students practice the strategy in pairs.

2. Block (1997) suggested the use of "reverse think alouds." In this strategy, students ask the teacher what he or she is thinking rather than the teacher telling the students. Students listen silently as the teacher reads. Then, the students stop the teacher during the reading to ask him/her questions. These questions might include such things as asking for predictions, describing a mental image, figuring out a difficult word or phrase from the context, clarifying the text, or summarizing the text.

Strategy 30: Think-Pair-Share

Title of Strategy: Think-Pair-Share

When to Use the Strategy:

- Pre-reading
- During reading
- Post-reading

Description of Strategy: Think-Pair-Share is a cooperative discussion strategy developed by Lyman (1981). The teacher poses a challenging or open-ended question and gives students between 30 and 60 seconds to think about the question silently. Students then pair with another student sitting nearby and discuss their ideas for 3 to 4 minutes. Then, the teacher asks for student comments or takes a classroom vote. Using this strategy, the responses received are often more intellectually concise, because students have had a chance to reflect on their ideas.

Purposes/Goals of Strategy:

- Provide an easy-to-follow structure to allow students to discuss text in a structured manner
- Allow students to process their own thinking both individually and with a partner
- Encourage students to elaborate on their own information and thinking in a low-anxiety environment with a partner

Teaching Students to Use the Strategy:

1. **Think.** The teacher sparks students' thinking with a question, prompt, or observation.

   The students should take 30 to 60 seconds just to THINK about the question.

2. **Pair.** Using designated partners, nearby neighbors, or a desk mate, students PAIR up to talk about the answer each came up with. They compare their mental or written notes and identify the answers they think are best, most convincing, or least common.
3. **Share.** After students talk in pairs for a few minutes, the teacher calls for pairs to SHARE their thinking with the rest of the class. The teacher can do this

by going around in round-robin fashion, calling on each pair, or by taking answers as they are called out (or as hands are raised). Often, the teacher or a designated helper will record these responses on the board or on the overhead.

Adapting this Strategy:

1. One variation of this structure is to skip the whole-class discussion.
2. Another variation is to have students write down their thoughts on index cards. This gives the instructor an opportunity to see whether there are problems in comprehension.

Strategy 31:
Three-Column IQR Sheet

Title of Strategy: Three-Column IQR Sheet

When to Use the Strategy:

- During reading

Description of Strategy: This technique will help students to elicit significant information and facts from the text, provide opportunities for questions, and think about their reactions, opinions, and feelings about the reading.

Purposes/Goals of Strategy:

- Identify significant information, main ideas, and facts from a selected text passage
- Identify student questions as students read
- Metacognitively think about individual reactions, opinions, and feelings regarding the reading

Teaching Students to Use the Strategy:

1. Students have a three-column form with three headings: Information, Questions, and Responses.
2. As students read a section of a selected text or chapter, they write down any piece of important information from their reading in the "Information" column.
3. As students write down the piece of information, they write a question that they have about it in the "Questions" column.
4. Then, they either search for the answer to their question and put it in the "Response" column or elaborate on their thinking in the "Response" column by noting their reactions, opinions, and feelings about the reading.
5. Students begin again with "Information" as they resume reading the selected text passage or chapter.

Adapting this Strategy:

1. This strategy could be adapted to be done in pairs or small groups to elicit discussion.
2. As students identify questions, they could be shared for a large group discussion by noting them on chart paper at the front of the room.

Strategy 32:
Three-Two-One (3-2-1)

Title of Strategy: Three-Two-One (3-2-1)

When to Use the Strategy:

- During reading
- Post-reading

Description of Strategy: The 3-2-1 strategy explained by Zygouris-Coe, Wiggins, and Smith (2004) gives students a chance to interact with the text by summarizing key ideas, thinking about what interests them in the reading, and then posing a question to clarify their understanding. Students fill out a piece of paper labeled "3-2-1" with "3 Things You Found Out," "2 Interesting Things," and "1 Question You Still Have." This strategy is versatile and depending upon what is being read, the teacher may wish to change what the "3-2-1" items stand for.

Purposes/Goals of Strategy:

- Reflect on concepts and ideas introduced in the text passage
- Identify what intrigues students in a reading
- Give students the opportunity to seek clarification

Teaching Students to Use the Strategy:

1. Using a pre-written chart or a blank index card, you will model for students how to use this strategy.
2. Write the first heading of "3 Things You Found Out." Have students go back through the text, verbally identifying, underlining, or highlighting three things they discovered. Then, have students verbally share out responses.
3. Continue modeling the next two parts of the chart.
4. Depending upon the language abilities of your students, you may wish to have them simply copy from the text or, alternatively, summarize what they read in their own words. As you model the strategy for the first time, emphasize what you want them to do.
5. After modeling, you can expect students to use this strategy on their own.

Adapting this Strategy:

1. This strategy can be collected as a "ticket out the door" where students complete this brief reading activity at the end of a daily reading.

2. Teachers may use this reading strategy and then go into "Think-Pair-Share" or other cooperative structures to begin a daily reading based on what was completed yesterday.
3. This strategy can be used to activate prior reading and followed by more complex reading strategies like creating an outline, plotting a Venn diagram, identifying sequences, or predicting what will happen next.

THINGS YOU FOUND OUT
3
INTERESTING THINGS
2
QUESTION YOU STILL HAVE
1

Figure 3.10 3-2-1 sample tool

Strategy 33:
Three-Minute Pause

Title of Strategy: Three-Minute Pause

When to Use the Strategy:

- During reading

Description of Strategy: The Three-Minute Pause helps students process information by providing a short break during which they summarize new content, connect new content to prior knowledge, and are free to ask clarifying questions. This strategy is currently promoted by Jay McTighe and Grant Wiggins (2004).

Purposes/Goals of Strategy:

- Reflect on concepts and ideas introduced in the text passage
- Make connections with prior knowledge or experience
- Give students the opportunity to seek clarification

Teaching Students to Use the Strategy:

1. **Summarize key ideas thus far.** The teacher instructs students to get into groups of three to five students. A total of three minutes is given for the entire process. First, the focus is on the key points of the lesson or reading up to this point. This pause allows the teacher to assess if the students are getting the main ideas.
2. **Add your own thoughts.** Next, the students consider prior knowledge connections they can make to the new information. Suggested questions might be: "what connections can be made?," "what does this remind you of?," "what would round out your understanding of this?," or "what can you add?"
3. **Pose clarifying questions.** Are there things that remain unclear? Are there confusing parts? Are you having difficulty making connections? Can you predict where we are headed? Can you dig for deeper meaning?

Adapting this Strategy:

1. You can do this as a writing assignment, in addition to a verbal activity.

Strategy 34:
Vocabulary Builder

Title of Strategy: Vocabulary Builder

When to Use the Strategy:

- Pre-reading
- During reading
- Post-reading

Description of Strategy: The Vocabulary Builder allows students to focus on individual vocabulary words and expand their language use.

Purposes/Goals of Strategy:

- Connect new vocabulary to prior vocabulary words
- Have students use target vocabulary words in a sentence
- Allow students to make a visual picture of the meaning of the word

Teaching Students to Use the Strategy:

1. Students fill in target vocabulary, using a grid such as that shown below.

Vocabulary Word

> *[Students write the new target vocabulary word here.]*

Definition

> *[Students write the definition of the*
> *vocabulary word in the target language.]*

_____

_____

_____

_____

Antonyms/Synonyms

_____

_____

_____

Sentence

[Students use the new target vocabulary word
in a sentence in the world language]

_____

_____

_____

<u>**Student Visual Picture**</u>

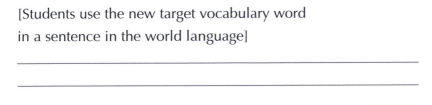

*[Students draw and color a picture of the
target vocabulary word here.]*

Figure 3.11 Vocabulary builder

Strategy 35:
Vocabulary Prediction Chart

Title of Strategy: Vocabulary Prediction Chart

When to Use the Strategy:

- Pre-reading
- During reading
- Post-reading

Description of Strategy: Students are given a list of words that they write on the chart and asked to predict the meaning of each word before reading the text. After reading, the students go back and write what they think the meaning of the word is.

Purposes/Goals of Strategy:

- Connect new vocabulary to prior vocabulary words
- Have students make predictions about unknown vocabulary
- Allow students to use clue words in the text to explain their guess

Teaching Students to Use the Strategy:

1. The students or the teacher write a list of vocabulary words in the first column.
2. Before reading the text, students write a prediction about what they think the word means.
3. After reading the text, students go back and write what they think the meaning of the word is, identifying clue words in the reading (along with page numbers) that helped them with the after-reading definition.

Vocabulary Word	Predicted Meaning	After Reading Definition	Clue Words and Corresponding Page Numbers of Clue Words from the Text

Figure 3.12 Vocabulary prediction chart

Strategy 36:
Vocabulary Question Organizer

Title of Strategy: Vocabulary Question Organizer

When to Use the Strategy:

● During reading

Description of Strategy: This strategy teaches students to ask questions about target vocabulary at different levels of understanding—i.e., knowledge, comprehension, application, analysis, and evaluation.

Purposes/Goals of Strategy:

● Answer questions at different levels of understanding to deepen students' understanding of the target vocabulary
● Discover and extend the meaning of challenging vocabulary words

Teaching Students to Use the Strategy:

1. The teacher copies a vocabulary grid for each student to use individually or has the students copy the grid from the chalkboard or an overhead.
2. This grid consists of five boxes with sentence prompts in each box to represent different levels of understanding.
3. One box is labeled "Target Vocabulary Word or Phrase in Context." In this box, either the teacher reads a sentence to the students to copy into this box or the teacher directs the students to copy a specific sentence with the target vocabulary from a text reading.
4. The teacher has the students label the other four boxes as "Comprehension," "Application," "Analysis," and "Evaluation."
5. For each of these four boxes, the teacher either writes or has students write a sentence starter that corresponds with each level of understanding. Some examples include:
   ● "Comprehension:" What do I believe this word means?
   ● "Application:" This vocabulary word is . . . _____ / This vocabulary is not . . . _____.
   ● "Analysis:" What parts of this word do I recognize from other words I know?
   ● "Evaluation:" Why is this word important for me to know?
6. Students work individually on filling out the four boxes listed above.

Adapting this Strategy:

1. This strategy could be done in small groups while the teacher circulates from group to group, monitoring their progress. Charts could then be debriefed in the full classroom setting at a designated time for students to share their responses. Each group could be responsible for the same target vocabulary word or phrase or different vocabulary words or phrases from the text.

Strategy 37:
Wordstorming

Title of Strategy: Wordstorming

When to Use the Strategy:

- Before reading

Description of Strategy: Wordstorming (Allen, 1999) is a technique used to find out what students already know about a concept and the words associated with it before reading a novel or a selection of a text. It uses a variety of word processing skills by activating prior knowledge.

Purposes/Goals of Strategy:

- Activate prior knowledge
- Develop multiple contexts for words
- Highlight relationships among words
- Identify, list, categorize, and label words
- Expose each student to what their thinking has in common and how their thinking is unique regarding words out of context

Teaching Students to Use the Strategy:

1. The teacher asks students individually to write down all the words they can think of related to a specific concept, theme, or target word in the upcoming text.
2. After students have written their word lists independently, have students work in pairs or in small groups.
3. Students work on combining their individual lists into categories of words with labels at the top for each of the word categories.
4. Students may have a category labeled "miscellaneous," but they may put no more than three words from their combined lists into this category.

Adapting this Strategy:

1. This activity could be done by having the teacher pull out important words from the upcoming text and having students categorize and label the words and try to guess the root word for the specific concept, theme, or target word.

4 Reading Activities

Reading Activities Use Chart

Activity Number	Name of Activity	Before Reading	During Reading	After Reading
1	Audio/Electronic/Computer Texts		X	
2	CliffsNotes		X	X
3	Comic Strips Using "Comic Creator"		X	X
4	Create a Test or Quiz			X
5	Cubing	X		X
6	Good and Better			X
7	Illustrated Visualizations	X		X
8	Inferencing Boxes	X	X	X
9	Jigsaw		X	
10	Key Word Compositions			X
11	Pictionary	X	X	X
12	Picture Sequencing		X	
13	Picture Talk	X		
14	Prove It!			X
15	Quick! Draw!			X
16	Radio News Broadcast			X
17	Read-Draw-Talk-Write		X	
18	Readers' Bookmarks	X	X	X
19	Reciprocal Teaching		X	X
20	Strip Story Pictures		X	X
21	Tic-Tac-Toe Choice Board			X
22	Think-Write-Pass			X
23	Vocabulary Blocks		X	X
24	Would You Bet On It?	X	X	
25	Word Walls	X	X	X
26	Y-Notes		X	X

Activity 1:
Audio/Electronic/Computer Texts

Title of Activity: Audio/Electronic/Computer Texts

When to Use the Activity:

- During reading

Description of Activity: For the Audio/Electronic/Computer Texts activity, students listen to commercially produced internet books or CDs while reading. This activity provides reading support to the students through oral reading, and the visual text while hearing the story facilitates reading growth.

Purposes/Goals of Activity:

- Increase students' comprehension
- Provide an accurate source of vocabulary and pronunciation
- Improve students' fluency
- Aid in word identification abilities

Ideas for Using the Activity:

1. A terrific online source for audio books is available through many libraries. It is called TumbleBook Library and has many children's books in various languages in an electronic book format.

These books integrate traditional print reading with some animation, music, narration, and some computer interactivity. TumbleBook Library allows readers to experience print reading with visual and/or interactive media.

There is an online collection of talking picture books, chapter books, and books for early readers. In addition, there are some read-along books with sentences highlighted as they are being read.

To access the TumbleBook Library, you may want to see if your local online library has these books available, or go to http://www.tumblebooks.com/library/asp/customer_login.asp?accessdenied=%2Flibrary%2Fasp%2Fhome%5Ftumbleb ooks%2Easp.

You can try out their free 30-day trial as a teacher once you register.

Another source is the International Children's Digital Library. This site has a wonderful collection of children's books from all over the world. Some of the books are in different languages. While you can access the books on this site for free, you can also become a volunteer, member, or sponsor to help this organization's mission to expand and maintain a digital library that best serves the world's children. As can be assumed, it requires ongoing investment in collection development, preservation, and software development. Go to http://en.childrenslibrary.org/.

Another source is YouTube. Go online and search for animated children's stories. You can spend so much time searching for lots of great materials. For example, you can find things like:

Fairy Tale: Three Little Pigs in Spanish (Los Tres Cerditos) from Speakaboos at https://www.youtube.com/watch?v=WkY7ASgzXTk

Turtle's Flute: Learn French with subtitles—Story for Children from BookBox. com at https://www.youtube.com/watch?v=-818b5vpPjc

The First Well: Learn German with subtitles—Story for Children from BookBox. com at https://www.youtube.com/watch?v=S0uTgSBdbUg

Adapting this Activity:

1. Teachers can use a projector to show an entire classroom the electronic book.
2. Students might use individual headphones to hear different electronic books.

Activity 2: CliffsNotes

Title of Activity: CliffsNotes

When to Use the Activity:

- During reading (the glossary stage)
- Post-reading (the summary and commentary stages)

Description of Activity: Students create their own CliffsNotes for a chapter of a novel and/or reading selection. They do so using the CliffsNotes format of summary, commentary, and glossary. The summary stage requires students to simply write a summary of the chapter/reading selection, either in English or in the target language. The commentary stage involves students documenting their observations about the reading, which can include, for example, an explanation of the author's purpose for writing the chapter/reading selection or a personal response to an occurrence and/ or character's actions in the reading. Last, students prepare a glossary of vocabulary words and their translations for a variety of purposes, like clarifying challenging and unfamiliar vocabulary, signaling vocabulary pertinent to the purpose/overall theme of the chapter (such as vocabulary related to a character's description), and listing recycled vocabulary from previous course work.

Purposes/Goals of Activity:

- Monitor comprehension of text during reading
- Serve as student-produced notes for class reference and use

Ideas for Using the Activity:

1. Because the product of the activity is in the form of CliffsNotes, the teacher could photocopy the student work (after review and revision) and distribute it to the class to use as notes of reference. Also, the student-produced CliffsNotes would serve as a useful study guide and review sheet.

Adapting this Activity:

1. Students can work through CliffsNotes in a jigsaw manner. The teacher could divide the class into three groups that each focus on only one of the Cliffs-Notes stages of summary, commentary, and glossary. Each group shares their work with the class, provides constructive feedback and/or suggestions for modifications/additions to the work, and then copies the other two groups' work on a notes sheet that outlines the CliffsNotes format.

Activity 3:
Comic Strips Using "Comic Creator"

Title of Activity: Comic Strips Using "Comic Creator"

When to Use the Activity:

- During reading
- Post-reading

Description of Activity: This free, easy-to-use website by read-write-teach allows teachers or students to easily create their own comic books. Comics can be one panel, two panels, three panels, or six panels in length. It is easy to add a comic title, people, talking balloons, and props to the website comics. Once completed, it is easy to save a digitized copy of the comic book or print hard copies.

Website URL: http://www.readwritethink.org/materials/comic/index.html

Pre-Planning PDF Sheet: http://www.readwritethink.org/lesson_images/lesson195/comic-strip-planning.pdf

Teachers and students may use this sheet to help pre-plan and revise their comic strip work.

Purposes/Goals of Activity:

- Create original comic strips using a web-based source
- Think analytically about characters, events, and themes of the reading
- Summarize text using visual cues
- Expand critical thinking by focusing on significant points in a text

Ideas for Using the Activity:

1. Teachers can create and use comic strips to encourage student writing.
2. Students can create comic strips to visually represent and summarize reading text.
3. Students can draw and write their own short stories.

Adapting this Activity:

1. *Hand-Drawn Comics or Storyboards*: If teachers or students do not want to use a website to create comics, students can write and hand draw storyboards to review reading text. As students complete a reading section or chapter, have students demonstrate their understanding of the reading by illustrating what happened. Teachers may wish for their students to simply illustrate the reading in a sequential four-box, six-box, or eight-box blank storyboard format, or

teachers might have students do the illustrations and then write a synopsis in the target language about what is happening in each storyboard block.

2. *Sentence Strips and/or Comics*: Once storyboards or comics are created, students can place sentence strips in the correct order regarding information from a chapter or selection. There are several variations to this activity:

   a. Have students put comics (without any written captions) in order as the teacher reads the story in the target language.

   b. Have the comic pictures and captions cut apart. Students put the cartoons in order and then put the correct pre-written caption underneath each picture.

   c. Have comic pictures with no captions. Students put the cartoon squares in order and then take turns telling their partner in the target language what is happening in each picture.

   d. Have pre-written captions but no comic pictures above the captions. Students put the captions written in the target language in the order of the story. Then, students have several minutes to draw illustrations above about what is happening in each comic picture.

   e. Have pre-drawn comic squares, but no written script, beneath each illustration. Have students write sentences for each comic square in the target language.

3. *Different Types of Comic Strip Creators*: ToonDoo.com is a new website that lets users easily create comic strips with pre-built or uploaded images and text. The creation tool is a Flash application that includes a number of options for characters, props, backgrounds, and text bubbles. Users can also upload their own images and include them in the comic strip. Once the strip is created it can also be published to the ToonDoo platform, along with a title, tags, and a description. You have to sign up if you want to create a comic strip. The service is currently free. Each comic strip comes with an RSS feed and Digg and del. icio.us submit links.

   Website URL: http://www.toondoo.com/toondoo/Home.toon
   Another Website URL: www.makebeliefscomix.com

Activity 4:
Create a Test or Quiz

Title of Activity: Create a Test or Quiz

When to Use the Activity:

- Post-reading

Description of Activity: Students identify important information in the reading and construct both questions and answers from the text that they think may be asked on an upcoming test or quiz. This activity measures both language use and comprehensibility of target reading.

Purposes/Goals of Activity:

- Discern essential information from reading
- Craft questions and answers from text
- Reread text to enhance comprehension

Ideas for Using the Activity:

1. Put students in pairs or small groups.
2. Assign students a section of the text or chapter to review.
3. Have students create both the questions and answers that they believe will be asked on a future test or quiz. Encourage students to make a variety of question types: multiple choice, matching, short answer, and essay.
4. The teacher can use the student-created questions and answers in a review game or as actual questions on an upcoming test or quiz.

Adapting this Activity:

1. Students could create a Jeopardy-type review game for the class.
2. Once students create questions and answers, various groups could present their questions to the class to see if other groups in the classroom can answer them.

Activity 5: Cubing

Title of Activity: Cubing

When to Use the Activity:

- Pre-reading
- Post-reading

Description of Activity: Cubing is a technique that can help students think at different levels of Bloom's taxonomy (Cowan & Cowan, 1980). It allows students to look at a single issue or topic from a variety of angles and develop multidimensional perspectives, rather than a singular one. The cubes are six-sided figures that have a different activity on each side of the cube. A student rolls the cube and performs the activity that comes up.

Purposes/Goals of Activity:

- Reinforce understanding of a reading
- Extend and/or demonstrate understanding of what was read
- Offer a variety of reading tasks that depend on the abilities and interests of students

Ideas for Using the Activity:

1. Students can work alone, in pairs, or in groups to roll the cube and perform the activities.
2. Students working in pairs or in groups can have the choice of rolling again if they do not like the activity that comes up.
3. Many suggestions for prompts to be written on the sides of the cube include:
    - describe it* connect it* illustrate it*
    - compare it* change it* rearrange it*
    - associate it* solve it* relate it to something else*
    - analyze it* question it* argue for/against it*

*Cube template: Cubing. Retrieved July 23, 2008 from http://curry.edschool. virginia.edu/files/nagc_cubing__think_dots.pdf (pp. 11–16).

Adapting this Activity:

*Teachers can create cube tasks that are differentiated in response to student readiness or student interest/learning profile.

1. To differentiate cubes in response to student readiness, two or more cubes could be created with the same commands but at different complexity levels. For example, two cubes could ask students to perform the skill of comparison at different levels of complexity. One cube may ask a student to compare the interests of a storybook character to the student's own interests whereas another cube may ask for a comparison between the storybook character's interest and the interests of a similar character who lived in a different time period.

2. To differentiate cubes in response to student interest or learning profile, the teacher assigns students to tables with cubes that match their specific interest or learning profile. For instance, visual learners would work with a cube designed with tasks such as drawing Venn diagrams, making models, organizing information with graphic organizers, and making charts. Oral learners would enjoy cubes with tasks that are more spoken in nature, such as telling a story, presenting for/against arguments, and role-playing.

Activity 6:
Good and Better

Title of Activity: Good and Better

When to Use the Activity:

- Post-reading

Description of Activity: Good and Better is a reading and writing activity that accelerates student writing and language development. Using texts that have been read to students or that they have read themselves, choose two sentences that exhibit excellent descriptive language. Those are the "better sentences." Keeping the same meaning and language patterns, students rewrite the sentences, substituting less expressive, precise, and engaging language. Those are the "good" sentences. Compile sentences in a two-chart outline, one chart for each kind of sentence.

Sample Chart

"Good"	"Better"
1. The noise scared me.	1. The unexpected, crashing noise startled me and made me jump.
2. Patricia goes to California.	2. Patricia flies internationally to California.

Purposes/Goals of Activity:

- Provide models of expressive and precise language in narrative and expository texts
- Produce internalization of excellent models of writing that can then be used as references for the student's own writing
- Increase the understanding of the role of effectiveness of descriptive adjectives and adverbs (vocabulary development)

Ideas for Using the Activity:

1. "Better" sentences are collected, and lists of their descriptive words and phrases are compiled and studied.
2. Teacher supplies a list of "good" sentences, and students work together using their individual and class vocabulary to make the sentences "better."
3. In peer review teams, students assess and edit their writing, coaching each other on the use of descriptive vocabulary.

Adapting this Activity:

1. The teacher and the class can review and recite the "good/better" sentences every class period for three to five days of the week, in order to reinforce vocabulary and syntax of the model sentences.

2. As a bell ringer activity in recall, students could transform the "good" sentences written on an overhead transparency into "better" sentences, and vice versa.

Activity 7:
Illustrated Visualizations

Title of Activity: Illustrated Visualizations

When to Use the Activity:

- During reading
- Post-reading

Description of Activity: Students are asked to create visual images as they hear a text read aloud. After the text is read aloud, the teacher explains and models what picture the teacher created in his/her head as the text was being read. Under the drawing, the teacher writes a sentence summarizing the picture. Then, the teacher reads another section aloud and guides the students in a discussion about what mental images they saw and helps students to construct summarizing sentences about their visual images. The teacher leads the classroom in a discussion about why people form different images in their minds and how individuals are influenced differently by the text and prior experiences.

Purposes/Goals of Activity:

- Create mental images while reading
- Visually summarize information about a text
- Use as a prompt for a literature discussion

Ideas for Using the Activity:

1. Teacher reads aloud in a large group, and then students are given a few minutes to draw and write about their visualizations.
2. Students could be directed to read a section of text on their own and to then draw/write about their visualizations.
3. Students could read text aloud, share visualizations, sketch pictures, and then be asked to find text support for their images.
4. As students read certain sections of text, they can use their drawings to spark discussions about the text.

Adapting this Activity:

1. Students could make a 9- or 10-page book in which they are asked to draw 9 or 10 times and summarize in the target language while independently reading a book.

Activity 8:
Inference Boxes

Title of Activity: Inference Boxes

When to Use the Activity:

- Pre-reading
- During reading
- Post-reading

Description of Activity: To infer is to combine schema and background knowledge with clues provided in the text to form a new idea. When students make inferences about a text, they draw conclusions based on reasoning. Inference boxes were devised as an activity in which students think about cause and effect relationships in the target language.

The instructor may assign inference boxes before, during, or after reading, depending on the goal of the activity. For example, an instructor that wants students to predict the vocabulary and grammar used to present concepts and ideas in a text would assign inference boxes before reading. The instructor would assign inference boxes during reading if the goal of the activity were for students to draw conclusions as they read.

Following is a sample worksheet for using inference boxes. In each box is either a cause or an effect. When a cause is listed, students brainstorm (pre-reading) or draw conclusions from the text (during reading/after reading) to find the effect, and vice versa.

Purposes/Goals of Activity:

- Predict concepts and ideas introduced in a text passage
- Brainstorm vocabulary and grammar likely to be found in the passage
- Construct cause and effect scenarios in the target language

Ideas for Using the Activity:

1. Differentiate the complexity of the inferences by making them into cards color-coded by difficulty.

Adapting this Activity:

1. Students can play "Inference Boxes" as a game.

Materials:

- Game board
- One die
- Inference cards, prepared ahead of time with a cause on one side and effect on the other side of the card

1. When I woke up, the streets were wet and power lines were down.	2. We turned our cell phones off and began eating popcorn.
Inference: It stormed last night.	Inference: We are at the movies.
3. I went to sleep past my bedtime last night.	4. A student yawns several times in class.
Inference: I woke up late.	Inference: The student is tired or bored.

Figure 4.1 Sample inference cards

Directions:

1. Students roll the die to figure out the order of turns. Highest roll goes first.
2. The first student rolls the die and the person to his/her left draws a card. *The student who draws the card may choose to read EITHER the cause side OR the effect side, which should detail both a cause and effect from the text read.* If the rolling student correctly phrases the cause or effect in the target language, s/he may move the number of spaces rolled. If the student does not answer correctly, s/he may not move.
3. First student to the finish line wins.

Start

Finish

Figure 4.2 Printable game template

Activity 9:
Jigsaw

Title of Activity: Jigsaw

When to Use the Activity:

- During reading

Description of Activity: Jigsaw is a task-specialization design in which the teacher assigns each student on a team a specialty in one aspect of a learning unit. Each student specializes in the assigned aspect, meets with students from other teams with the corresponding aspect, and after mastering the material returns to his/her team to teach teammates (Kagan, 1992).

Purposes/Goals of Activity:

- Master a reading selection
- Summarize a reading selection in one's own words, in the target language
- Discuss a reading selection in the target language
- Provide a means for students to teach, and review with, other students assigned reading selections

Ideas for Using the Activity:

1. The Jigsaw method can be used when reading and discussing cultural readings, both in English and in the world language.
2. Teachers can assign Jigsaw readings for short stories in the target language.

Adapting this Activity:

1. Team Jigsaw: All students on a team of four become experts on one topic and then spread out to share their new knowledge with the rest of the class. For example, in a class of six teams a novel chapter is divided into three parts and two teams are assigned to each part.

Activity 10:
Key Word Compositions

Title of Activity: Key Word Compositions

When to Use the Activity:

- Post-reading

Description of Activity: Students use selected words from a text to compose key ideas in sentence or paragraph form. Students are given a number of words related to, or used in, key ideas of the reading. Using a standard number of three words per sentence, students compose sentences in the target language that summarize key events of the passage. The three words can be arranged in any order and changed to observe correct target language grammar. Also, extra words can certainly be added for concise sentences.

Purposes/Goals of Activity:

- Build confidence in writing by providing a starting point for writing
- Help the student build a subject area "voice" through words from a particular subject or content
- Students of different abilities and styles can find their own voice

Ideas for Using the Activity:

1. The teacher could extend the activity to a homework assignment in order to reinforce and expand on the vocabulary. An example of an assignment would be for students to draw five pictures in a story format and, under each picture, write at least two sentences in, for example, Spanish that describe the picture with the focus vocabulary from the key word compositions activity.

Adapting this Activity:

1. Students work with two different lists of vocabulary that relate to the key ideas of the reading passage. One list could include more advanced vocabulary for readers with a wider range of target vocabulary knowledge, and the other could include more common, higher-frequency vocabulary.

Activity 11:
Pictionary

Title of Activity: Pictionary

When to Use the Activity:

- Pre-reading
- During reading
- Post-reading

Description of Activity: Pictionary is a game produced by Western Publishing Company, Inc. This game is literally charades on paper. Students will try to get their classmates to guess a target language word or phrase by correctly drawing pictures.

Purposes/Goals of Activity:

- Serve as a visual source for vocabulary
- Have students practice vocabulary in a nonlinguistic format

Ideas for Using the Activity:

1. Split the class into two teams.
2. Randomly determine which team will go first and how many points are needed for a team to win.
3. One student from the team to go first will go to the chalkboard.
4. The teacher shows the student a word or phrase in the target language.
5. Then, a timer is set and the student tries to draw a visual representation of the word or phrase for his or her teammates to guess before the time is up for the team. (The student drawing cannot use any gestures, actions, words, numbers, or letters with their visual drawing.)
6. If the team guesses the word or phrase correctly before time is up, the team gets a point.
7. Now, the opposite team takes its turn.
8. The first team to get the predetermined number of points wins the game.

Adapting this Activity:

1. Students can play this game as a whole class or in small groups using pen and paper or whiteboards.

Activity 12:
Picture Sequencing

Title of Activity: Picture Sequencing

When to Use the Activity:

- During reading

Description of Activity: Students are given pictures of events of the story that they put in order as they read the text.

Purposes/Goals of Activity:

- Document student understanding of the text
- Pinpoint sections of the text that are confusing for students

Ideas for Using the Activity:

1. Students use picture sequencing as a self-check of their understanding of the reading. Students read the passage, sequence the pictures, and then compare their sequenced pictures with another student's work.
2. The teacher assigns students a passage to read in pairs. Pairs work together to read, comprehend, and sequence the pictures.
3. Students listen to a recording of the reading and sequence pictures as they hear the pictured detail being read.

Adapting this Activity:

1. A worksheet with pictures presented out of order can be prepared ahead of time, which students simply number as they sequence them in order. Preparing a worksheet avoids the extra work of making class sets of pictures.
2. When presenting a reading through a spoken recording, the teacher can provide some students with a script of the reading, in order to facilitate the picture-sequencing activity. Doing so differentiates the process through which students comprehend and work with the text.

Activity 13:
Picture Talk

Title of Activity: Picture Talk

When to Use the Activity:

- Pre-reading

Description of Activity: The teacher selects key vocabulary words and/or phrases from the reading and creates an attractive presentation for the words, like presenting the words with pictures from word art. The words and phrases selected should give an indication of the plot of the reading. Students then write a short story of a couple sentences using the words. Students should find that their pre-reading story inventions follow a similar, or the same, storyline as that of the selected reading.

Purposes/Goals of Activity:

- Anticipate main ideas, key concepts, and important details in a reading
- Reduce needed information efficiency from a text
- Strengthen students' reading comprehension

Ideas for Using the Activity:

1. The teacher could present the activity as a competition to see which student teams can invent stories in which details align closest to the reading selection.

Adapting this Activity:

1. The class keeps track of the number of sentences that align with the plot of the selected reading. Students can orally invent sentences based on the key vocabulary words/phrases that the teacher writes on an overhead transparency. Then, as students read the text, they can go to the overhead to cross off details generated from Picture Talk that match details in the reading itself.

Activity 14:
Prove It!

Title of Activity: Prove It!

When to Use the Activity:

- Post-reading

Description of Activity: Students read a series of statements in the target language that correctly or incorrectly summarizes a detail or event of the reading. They must determine if the statement is true or false based on what they read and determine if the statement is clearly supported in the text or believed to be true even though it is not stated word-for-word. Then, students document their findings in one of two ways. For statements clearly presented in the text, students find and record the page and paragraph number where the statement is found. For statements inferred as being true, students find a sentence or sentences in the text that support the inferred statement and write them as their answer.

Purposes/Goals of Activity:

- Recall what is read
- Distinguish between what a text says and what one can infer from the text
- Draw conclusions based on what is read

Ideas for Using the Activity:

1. Prove It! can be assigned as homework or a quiz.
2. The teacher can assign the activity as a collaborative group exercise. Students are put into groups of four, every member of the group being assigned two statements to prove/disprove. Each member then shares his/her proofs with teammates, who confirm or question the proofs before submitting the work.

Adapting this Activity:

1. Assign the reverse task: the students write a series of statements in the target language that correctly or incorrectly summarizes details or events of the reading, which they exchange with other classmates who will prove or disprove the statements.

Activity 15:
Quick! Draw!

Title of Activity: Quick! Draw!

When to Use the Activity:

- Post-reading

Description of Activity: Research shows that between 40 and 50 per cent of what one reads is forgotten after 15 minutes from reading. Quick! Draw! is a post-reading activity that encourages readers to review and remember what they read. It is a game that divides students into two teams within which one student draws a picture of something from the story and his teammates guess what it is. If the team guesses correctly, it wins a point and draws again. If the team guesses incorrectly, the point and opportunity to draw goes to the opposing team.

Purposes/Goals of Activity:

- Reciting aloud promotes concentration and provides time for the memory trace to consolidate
- Ensure that facts and events are remembered accurately

Ideas for Using the Activity:

1. Quick! Draw! can be the closure of a reading lesson or serve as a review game before a test.
2. Teachers can use the activity as a means of formative assessment to gather information about student comprehension and retention.
3. Students can draw story details on white boards.

Adapting this Activity:

1. Instead of dividing a class into two teams, teachers can create four or five smaller teams that each play Quick! Draw! simultaneously. Within each team, students rotate members to select and draw story details while the others compete to guess the drawing.
2. The teacher could prepare drawing cues ahead of time and distribute them to each group. That way, the groups will be assured to review the focal points of the reading that the instructor finds most important.

Activity 16:
Radio News Broadcast

Title of Activity: Radio News Broadcast

When to Use the Activity:

● Post-reading

Description of Activity: Working in groups, students will develop a short script for a radio news broadcast that illustrates concepts from a selected reading. Students will practice dramatizing their radio news broadcast and interviewing characters from the text in small groups and then share their presentation with the class. Dramatic presentation instruction has a stronger effect than verbal and visual instruction both immediately after the instruction and even 12 months later (Marzano et al., 2001, p. 131).

Purposes/Goals of Activity:

● Dramatize information from text
● Develop script from the text that illustrates concepts and interviews characters from the text
● Reread text to enhance comprehension

Ideas for Using the Activity:

1. Put students in small groups.
2. Identify a certain text or chapter and ask students to develop a short script for a radio news broadcast to illustrate what happened in the text.
3. Students create a script, incorporating interviews with characters from the script.
4. Students present their radio broadcast to the other groups in the class.

Adapting this Activity:

1. Each group of students could do the same text passage or chapter.
2. Each group of students could do a different text passage or chapter.

Activity 17:
Read-Draw-Talk-Write

Title of Activity: Read-Draw-Talk-Write

When to Use the Activity:

- During reading

Description of Activity: Read-Draw-Talk-Write is a cooperative activity in which readers express what they learn from what they read through drawing, speaking, and writing. First, the class establishes partnerships. Then, the teacher assigns a reading to the class. After individually reading the selection, students close the book and begin drawing a representation of what they read. When the teacher calls for time, partners show each other their drawings and talk about what they read. On a reading log sheet, partners then write a short summary of what they read.

Purposes/Goals of Activity:

- Read with attention to meaning
- Purposefully read (reread) to represent the information visually
- Self-monitor for comprehension ("what do I really understand?")
- Recall what was read without referring to text
- Write information in own words rather than copying from text

Ideas for Using the Activity:

1. Teachers can differentiate the activity by adjusting the manner in which students document communication. For example, students further along in their language competency can talk and write about their observations in the target language while other students do the same but in their native language. Furthermore, students can be given the option of documenting in the target or native language, according to their level of comfort regarding either task.

Adapting this Activity:

1. The "drawing" step can be omitted (in the event of time restraints), thus shortening the activity to Read-Talk-Write.

Activity 18:
Readers' Bookmarks

Title of Activity: Readers' Bookmarks

When to Use the Activity:

- Pre-reading
- During reading
- Post-reading

Description of Activity: For this activity, the teacher distributes small slips of blank paper that can be tucked into a book and used for making predictions, drawing visual representations, asking questions, or writing responses.

Purposes/Goals of Activity:

- Check for student understanding
- Make personal connections with text
- Pose questions for clarifying information with the teacher
- Use as "ticket in" or "ticket out" the door for formative assessment

Ideas for Using the Activity:

1. Bookmarks can be used to make predictions about an upcoming text.
2. Students can write what was important about the daily reading.
3. Students can use this as a communication tool with the teacher to ask questions or to request clarification about the reading.
4. Students can write down three "new" vocabulary words from the reading and the definitions in the target language.
5. Students can use the bookmarks to write responses to the literature reading.
6. Students can illustrate the bookmarks according to the daily reading.

Adapting this Activity:

1. Instead of using bookmarks, students can design book covers, complete with illustrations, a new title, and a synopsis of the book on the back of the book cover in the target language.

Activity 19:
Reciprocal Teaching

Title of Activity: Reciprocal Teaching

When to Use the Activity:

- During reading
- Post-reading

Description of Activity: Palincsar & Brown (1984) developed Reciprocal Teaching, which is a scaffolded discussion technique built on four strategies that good readers use to comprehend text: predicting, questioning, clarifying, and summarizing. Reciprocal Teaching combines the use of cooperative and collaborative learning in a multiple reading format. The teacher first models the four comprehension strategies. Students then practice the strategies in small groups. Reciprocal Teaching is a research-proven activity for teaching multiple comprehension strategies (Oczuks, 2003).

Purposes/Goals of Activity:

- Acquire comprehension strategies
- Help students become metacognitive about their reading
- Practice reading strategies with authentic text
- Scaffold instruction
- Provide peer support for learning
- Promote student social interaction and collaboration

Ideas for Using the Activity:

1. Before students begin to use Reciprocal Teaching, they need to have been taught and to have had time to practice the skills of summarizing, questioning, clarifying, and predicting. Teachers need to explicitly teach and model these four strategies.
2. Once students understand and are able to apply all four strategies, put students in groups of four.
3. Assign each student a role: summarizer, questioner, clarifier, and predictor.
4. One of the four is selected to be "the teacher of the group." His/her job is to facilitate the group's task, progress, and time management.
5. The students read a few paragraphs of an assigned text selection. Students use note-taking strategies, such as post-it notes or a four-column chart with each

column headed by one of the four comprehension activities. Students individually write down annotations of their assigned role.

6. After everyone has time to work individually, the "teacher of the group" facilitates a discussion.

- The summarizer highlights the key ideas in a summary-question format.
- The questioner asks the group questions about the text selection, including concerns about unclear parts, puzzling information, connections to previous concepts, the true intent of the characters in the story, etc.
- The clarifier helps the group address the confusing parts of the text through questions and helps the group answer questions from the questioner.
- The predictor offers future questions to the group about the upcoming text and shares guesses about what the author will share in the upcoming text and what events might happen next.

During the discussion, the "teacher of the group" encourages each student to cite reference points in the text that are the focus of the questions and/or evidence to support their discussion points.

7. As the discussion ensues, students add points from the other three roles to their post-it notes or column sheet to help create a deeper understanding of the text.

8. The classroom teacher circulates around the room to visit each group's discussion. He/she might ask a follow-up question to enrich the discussion.

Adapting this Activity:

1. The teacher may wish to start with very short readings to allow students to practice their skills before moving on to longer readings.

2. The teacher may want to show students a four-column mode or graphic organizer in which the four roles of summarizer, questioner, clarifier, and predictor have sample questions from a short reading that could be asked to the group as a model before small group work begins.

Activity 20:
Strip Story Pictures

Title of Activity: Strip Story Pictures

When to Use the Activity:

- During reading
- Post-reading

Description of Activity: For this activity, the teacher distributes small pictures of a story, or part of a story, in a baggie. Students must put the pictures into the correct order as to what happens in the story. After students reorder the pictures into the correct story order (and the teacher checks for correct order), students in pairs can take turns telling the story in their own words (using the target language) to each other. After students practice telling the story to their partners, the teacher can call on students to tell parts of the story to the class.

Purposes/Goals of Activity:

- Check for student understanding
- Give students a chance to practice target story vocabulary
- Use as "ticket in" or "ticket out" the door for formative assessment

Ideas for Using the Activity:

1. Sentence story strips can be used to check for larger chapter information or certain text passage information.
2. The teacher can create the illustrated story strips or students can draw and illustrate the pictures.
3. This activity could be done using only visual pictures OR the teacher could use separate pictures and separate written text. Students could first order the pictures and then order the written text under each picture.
4. Sentence story pictures could be used for students to work in small groups to create their own story, using target vocabulary and grammatical structures.

Adapting this Activity:

1. Students could draw and add a "new scene" to the current strip story pictures. This could either be just a picture or a picture with writing in the target language.

Activity 21:
Tic-Tac-Toe Choice Board

Title of Activity: Tic-Tac-Toe Choice Board

When to Use the Activity:

- Post-reading

Description of Activity: The teacher offers a choice board, designed like a tic-tac-toe board, in which students have the opportunity to choose options to practice skills and enhance study. Sample choices listed on a board menu may include verb practice, answering/forming questions, vocabulary development, identifying story details as true or false, or English-to-target language/target language-to-English translations. Students are allotted time to choose and work on the various tasks offered in the menu. When time is up, the teacher divides the class into two teams

Sample choice board:

Translate to Spanish. The shepherd does not laugh because he is furious. The sheep jumps and runs fast.	*Translate to English.* La oveja come al padre del señor Stevens. El papá del señor Stevens comió un pastor que llora como un bebé furioso.	*Draw the meaning of the story detail.* Ella llora despacio y salta sin las piernas.
Circle the word that does not belong. grita camina llora la oveja corre salta come	*Translate to Spanish aloud with a partner.* Monday the wolf eats. Thursday my dad cries. Saturday the girl sings. Wednesday the boy laughs and eats sheep.	*True or False?* 1. La oveja grita y el pastor corre. 2. El pastor está furioso porque la oveja canta mucho.
Unscramble the following phrases from the story vocabulary. erí nua zev ad nua tuelva ods sevec	*¿Cómo se dice en inglés:* La familia triste llora porque la oveja comió su lobo con las manos.	*Identify the grammar mistakes in the following phrases.* 1. La oveja está furioso. 2. El pastor grito.

Figure 4.3 Sample tic-tac-toe choice board: Spanish

that compete in the game of tic-tac-toe, earning chances to mark a square with their designated letter by correctly completing the given task aloud.

Purposes/Goals of Activity:

- Provide students with choices as to how they demonstrate knowledge of a reading
- Motivate students to recall what they read through game and competition
- Encourage students of different ability levels to work together and also individually contribute to a team goal

Ideas for Using the Activity:

1. Choice boards make fun bell ringers!
2. Make copies of the tasks and grid on overhead transparencies.
3. Several choice boards can be made and played throughout a period, as a review for a test on a longer reading or novel.

Adapting this Activity:

1. Instead of a tic-tac-toe design, a Connect Four game can be used. Instead of completing tasks to occupy squares on a tic-tac-toe grid, students complete tasks to earn the chance to drop alternating colored discs into a four-column, four-row grid, with the objective being the first team to connect four single-colored discs in a row—vertically, horizontally, or diagonally. For every time that a team answers correctly a task during a turn, the team chooses where to "drop" a colored disc in the grid.

   *For discs, you can purchase multicolored, transparent chips or use objects with varying shapes, like dice (square shape for one team) and pennies (circular shape for the opposing team).
   *Use the top portion of the overhead transparency to list the tasks that students must complete OR type a worksheet with the tasks on it to give to students.

Connect Four!

Figure 4.4

Activity 22:
Think-Write-Pass

Title of Activity: Think-Write-Pass

When to Use the Activity:

- Post-reading

Description of Activity: Think-Write-Pass is a post-reading activity that encourages students to reflect on what they learned from the reading. It requires several large pieces of paper.

1. Place a different subject heading at the top of each piece of chart paper. The heading could be a character, place, or important event from the text.
2. Have each group brainstorm and write down what they know about the topic.
3. The group passes the paper to another group.
4. The second group reads all that has been written, then writes down what else they know about the topic. *If the group is unable to add any original information, they should be encouraged to rephrase (using circumlocution) what is already noted.
5. The second group passes the paper to another group, who also adds to the sheet.
6. The process continues until all groups have contributed to all subjects.
7. *On the last pass, the group finds references for the statements on the chart paper.
8. Instruct students to place a page number and/or source beside each reference.
9. Share and post all the papers.

Purposes/Goals of Activity:

- Recall what is read
- Assess student understanding of text
- Peers provide peers with feedback about text

Ideas for Using the Activity:

1. Paper passing makes a great lesson closure.
2. Ask students in each group to write their contribution in a different colored pencil/marker and to include on the chart paper a color-coded key that identifies who wrote with which color. You will raise student accountability by doing so.

Adapting this Activity:

1. "Draw it! Draw it!" is an adaptation of paper passing. Instead of groups writing down information and passing the group chart paper to another group for additions, they draw parts of the scene together. Draw it! involves partners discussing and coming to a consensus on an important scene from the text and communicating it through pictures. The activity looks as follows when broken down into steps:

    1. Each set of partners needs a large piece of poster paper and one marker.
    2. Partners discuss and come to a consensus on an important scene from the story.
    3. After deciding, the first student starts the drawing.
    4. The second student adds to the picture.
    5. The partners swap the marker back and forth until the picture is complete.
    6. Partners share their picture and describe how it can be used as a visual reminder of their elected story scene.
    7. Students can also be instructed to write facts learned about the topic around the picture, in the target language.

Activity 23:
Vocabulary Blocks

Title of Activity: Vocabulary Blocks

When to Use the Activity:

- During reading
- Post-reading

Description of Activity: Students focus on new vocabulary in text and create memory linkages to help remember the vocabulary. In this activity, the student identifies the word, defines the word, writes an antonym or non-example, and draws a visual representation of the word.

Purposes/Goals of Activity:

- Create memory devices to remember new target vocabulary
- Visually represent the vocabulary word
- Identify the word by linking it with an antonym or non-example

Ideas for Using the Activity:

1. Students receive a piece of paper with several blocks on it (or fold a large sheet of paper to create multiples of four blocks).
2. Vocabulary words go in the upper left corner of each block, with a short definition in the box directly below it.
3. In the upper right corner goes an antonym (opposite meaning or non-example).
4. In the lower right corner, the student illustrates a drawing of the definition of the word.

Emaciated	Fat
Thin or bony	Student draws an illustration of "emaciated"

Figure 4.5 Sample blocks

Adapting this Activity:

1. The teacher may wish to take each student's drawings and photocopy them onto a new piece of paper, which can be used to test the students. Give them their photocopied drawings with a list of vocabulary words; students must then match each drawing with its corresponding word.

Activity 24:
Would You Bet On It?

Title of Activity: Would You Bet On It?

When to Use the Activity:

- Pre-reading
- During reading

Description of Activity: Would You Bet On It? is an active reading strategy that asks students to make a prediction about the outcome of a reading selection. The teacher presents possible scenarios that could occur with the characters of a reading selection and students, on the back of a one-sided, photocopied currency (from a foreign country), write a prediction (in English or in the target language) as to which scenario will actually happen. Students submit their predictions as "bets" that their chosen scenario will follow the outcome in the reading. The opportunities exist to win back lost money (for incorrect predictions) in order to bet again or to exchange a winning bet for a prize, like a homework pass.

Purposes/Goals of Activity:

- Promote interest in the reading
- Set a framework for reading
- Encourage students to focus when reading

Ideas for Using the Activity:

1. Teachers can teach a mini-lesson on currency conversions before using the activity for reading a text.

Adapting this Activity:

1. Instead of the teacher presenting possible outcomes from which to choose, a single, open-ended question about how an outcome may result could be presented.
2. Instead of students submitting their bets to the teacher, they could exchange them with a classmate. If the prediction statement is correct, the classmate would return the money back to the student who wrote it. If the prediction statement is incorrect, the classmate would keep the money.

Activity 25:
Word Walls

Title of Activity: Word Walls

When to Use the Activity:

- Pre-reading
- During reading
- Post-reading

Description of Activity: The Word Walls activity is a valuable way to integrate vocabulary, reinforce vocabulary, and have that vocabulary readily accessible to the students. A word wall is built on the spiral theory of mastery—repetition reinforces vocabulary and regular use of a word wall allows students to recycle many words. Teachers can set up word walls so that a different background color would coordinate with a thematic, topical, alphabetic, or organized theme so it doesn't become too random or overwhelming for students to follow. Word walls can serve as a working dictionary or verb conjugation reminder for students.

Purposes/Goals of Activity:

- Serve as a visual source for vocabulary
- Provide repetition for students of target vocabulary
- Recycle previous vocabulary

Ideas for Using the Activity:

1. *Idea #1:* Put a word wall in a prominent place in the classroom so that the teacher can refer to it often throughout various classes as part of his/her assignments.
2. *Idea #2—"Buzz" Game:* Have a file box of word cards with one index card for every word on the word wall. For every 15 cards in the box, place one card with the word "Buzz" written on it in the target language. Mix all the cards together so that the word wall words and the various "Buzz" cards are randomly mixed together. For the actual game, one at a time, have the students pull a card, show the card to the class, and say aloud the word on the card. If a student says the word correctly, he or she gets to keep the card. If the word is read incorrectly, the card is put back into the box. (Alternative: you might have the student give a definition of the word.) If the student pulls the "Buzz" card, he or she must put all the cards he or she has gathered up to this point back into the box. When allotted time for the game has expired (perhaps 10 or 15 words), the student holding the most cards is the winner. (Alternative: you

might have several game sets of cards and have the students play the game in small groups instead.)

3. *Idea #3—"Guess the Word" Game:* The class is divided into two teams. One student from one team comes to the front of the class and sits in a designated seat with his or her back to the chalkboard. A classmate from the other team selects a word from the word wall and writes the word on the chalkboard so the class can see it but the student cannot. The student in the designated seat who cannot see the word has the job of trying to guess the word by asking questions of the class to help him or her identify the selected word. Keep a tally of the number of questions or clues it takes for the student to guess the word. Then, another student on the opposite team takes his or her turn. (Alternative: this activity can be done as a whole-class activity or, if students are taught how to play the game, it might be done in several small groups at the same time with different words.)

Adapting this Activity:

1. Students can also keep a word wall page in their notebooks or writing folders, adding to the page as new vocabulary is introduced.

2. Students can keep a personal word wall page in their notebooks for vocabulary that they have discovered or would like to remember through independent reading or other classroom activities besides the vocabulary introduction in class.

3. Word walls can be made up of frequently used words or higher-level words like "million-dollar words" to enrich or enhance vocabulary.

4. If having a word wall is a challenge in class due to space constraints, you can also have "word ceilings" where the words are posted on the ceilings instead of the walls.

5. The teacher can attach words to the wall by using Velcro or pushpins. He/she can also use magnets on a white board.

6. The teacher can choose to have a student write the word on a long index card or piece of long construction paper.

Activity 26:
Y-Notes

Title of Activity: Y-Notes

When to Use the Activity:

- During reading
- Post-reading

Description of Activity: Y-Notes is an activity that can be used to help students discern similarities and differences between two topics of study. In the world language class, y-notes are useful when comparing and contrasting cultures.

Purposes/Goals of Activity:

- Discern similarities and differences between two topics of study
- Record organized notes as a precursor to writing a structured and organized comparison/contrast essay/summary

Ideas for Using the Activity:

1. Students can use the y-notes organizer as a note-taking technique.
2. Students can compare/contrast foreign countries with the United States via y-notes.
3. Students can use the y-notes organizer as a pre-writing activity for a comparison/contrast essay.

Example:

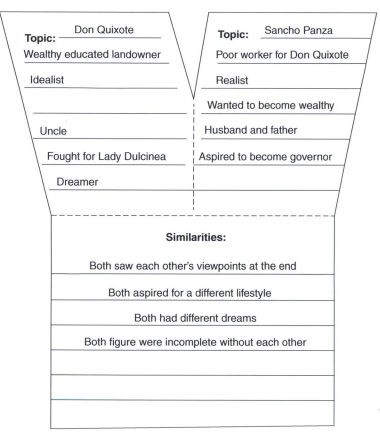

Figure 4.6 Y-notes blank organizer

Adapting this Activity:

1. Teachers can use the y-notes as an assessment piece. The teacher could fill in the various parts of the graphic organizer with correct and incorrect information regarding the focus topics, which students would evaluate and reorganize according to the facts that they learned.

5 Reader's Theater

What Is Reader's Theater?

Reader's Theater is reading done aloud to tell a story through words. Students read from a script and the character reading parts are divided among different readers. Readers are usually seated while reading from a script that is held in their hands or placed on a music stand in front of them. Students are not required to memorize, create costumes, make puppets, have extravagant student acting, or have a special stage unless you or the students wish to add such. Reader's Theater offers the interest level of theatrical productions but without a fully staged production with sets, costumes, full memorization, and staged dramatic action.

Benefits of Reader's Theater

Reader's Theater is a technique to help build strong reading and comprehension skills in students. Reader's Theater is a fluency building strategy that is engaging and entertaining to students as they work on practicing and improving their reading skills. The "presentation" of the reading isn't as important as the "rehearsal." It is through repetition and rehearsal that words and phrases that might be beyond a reader's reading level can be more easily assimilated into the reader's working vocabulary. Students absorb the words through repetition in Reader's Theater, but unlike long lists of vocabulary or drill activities, students are more focused and engaged because of the story and presentation element of Reader's Theater.

This is a versatile teaching technique that has a number of implementation forms. Teachers may use this dramatic technique to add interest, fun, and meaning to classroom activities through oral reading activities. In addition, teachers can use Reader's Theater as a reading resource approach to give information, teach facts, share ideas, or practice reading and language concepts.

One of the key components of Reader's Theater is to build fluency through the use of modeling. In modeling, students listen to more advanced text than they can read independently. This is important because students have a higher listening comprehension than reading comprehension. As a result, to increase reading ability and fluency, one way to accomplish this is to have students listen to richer and more complex vocabulary and more advanced text formats than they are able to read independently.

Implementing Reader's Theater

There are numerous ways to implement Reader's Theater as a reading resource approach or as a performance rehearsal process. Four reading resource approaches include participation storytelling, circle reading, read alouds, and cooperative reading.

Activity 1:
Participation Storytelling

For: Early World Language Reading Groups

When students are at initial world language reading levels, it is important to choose or to write scripts that feature high-frequency words and phrases that are repeated throughout the reading.

In this activity, the teacher is the primary narrator and the students participate by reading or reciting simple words, phrases, chants, and/or repeated lines. This method is similar to reading done in primary grades where students learning how to read assist the storyteller by listening and repeating information on cue from the teacher.

Implementation Steps:

Step 1: Copy and distribute the script to ALL students.

It is important that ALL students (even those without individual parts) are given a copy of the script, because the script contains the actual words of the story and helps the students relate the visual story they see and hear to the written words on the page.

Step 2: The teacher (or other main narrator) reads the script aloud to the students, and all students are encouraged to join in reciting repetitive words and phrases marked "All" on the script.

Step 3: Have students underline or highlight the "All" lines.

Step 4: For individual character parts, assign, or ask for, volunteers. (You want to be sure that more difficult parts do not go to the weaker students for the first few readings of the script.)

Step 5: Have individual readers underline or highlight their parts in a different color from the "All" lines.

Step 6: Practice reading the story aloud several times, including all solo and choral readers with their assigned parts.

Adapting this Activity:

1. Add some dramatic verbal inflection to the reading, simple stage directions, or props.
2. Have students illustrate the scripts, using a blank storyboard format. Students might draw and color pictures and then write the dialogue underneath the pictures.

3. For students with slower writing abilities, the storyboards could already have the information written in the target language underneath the blank squares. Students would read the sentences, draw a picture, and then color it in.

4. Using the ideas in #2 and #3 above, students could take home their storyboards and reread the stories to parents or other family members. Students could get a signature on a signature card to show that this was completed as homework.

5. Just using the script, students could take home the written script and reread it to parents or other family members. Students could get a signature on a signature card to show that this was completed as homework.

6. You can have students swap parts and reread the scripts over and over in class to practice the vocabulary and get additional reading repetition practice.

Activity 2:
Circle Reading

For: Early World Language Reading Groups

With this activity, students read all the different role parts available in the pre-written scripts. Students get to experiment, using different dramatic voices and practicing different language structures and vocabulary in a non-competitive, non-threatening environment.

Implementation Steps:

Step 1: Copy and distribute the script to ALL students.

Step 2: Have the students read silently through the entire script.

Step 3: After all students have read through the story silently, have all students sit in a large group to complete the next four steps.

Step 4: Have the student on the right read the first reader's part in the script. Then, have the next person read the second reader's part, and so on until the entire script is read. Simply continue around the circle. Do not assign any individual parts at this point.

Step 5: Then, debrief with the students regarding the reader parts in the scripts.
- What might each character sound like?
- What personalities do you think they have?
- How might each character act?
- What kind of gestures or body language might they use as they speak different parts?

Step 6: Next, discuss the importance of having a good narrator in the story.
- Narrators are important to introduce the story.
- Good narrators use effective voice inflections.
- Narrators are important to fill in all narrative details.
- Narrators set the mood for the story action.
- Narrators help the individual characters set the reading pace and sometimes cue the reader characters.

Step 7: Review the meanings and pronunciation of any difficult words with the students.

Step 8: Ask your readers to volunteer for specific reading parts. Have volunteers underline or highlight their lines and then read the script aloud again. Then, exchange parts around the circle and continue to read.

Adapting this Activity:

1. Instead of completing step 8 with the entire class, break students into smaller groups and have the individual groups assign and read specific parts. Select a narrator for each group and have him or her help with the assignment of reader roles and the reading in individual groups.

2. After students practice in small groups, have a competition between the smaller groups where they present their dramatic readings to the entire class. This encourages students to be more dramatic, along with giving additional vocabulary practice and repetition for the students.

Activity 3:
Read Alouds

For: Early World Language Reading Groups

This is a quick technique to get students involved in a meaningful reading activity and can be easily done at the beginning or end of class, or to focus students.

Implementation Steps:

Step 1: Copy and distribute the script to ALL students or ask them to share scripts in pairs.

Step 2: Have students read through the scripts silently or have the teacher read the script aloud.

Step 3: Ask for volunteers, or assign parts to various students in the class. Have the students underline or highlight their assigned lines. Have each student write his/her character's name at the top of the script.

Step 4: Have the assigned readers read the story aloud from their seats. Ask the readers to make any notes or pronunciation aids on their scripts.

Step 5: When the reading is completed, discuss the story, reading, and acting with the class.

Step 6: Reassign student parts and have the first character swap scripts with the second character so the next person reading has the highlighted script with any written notes or pronunciation aids. As students continue to change parts, they can exchange scripts.

Activity 4:
Cooperative Reading

For: Early World Language Reading Groups

This technique allows students to work in cooperative reading groups and take ownership to assign parts, suggest improvements, and make additions or changes to the presentation.

Implementation Steps:

Step 1: Copy and distribute the script to ALL students or ask them to share scripts in pairs.

Step 2: Assign students into cooperative reading groups.

Step 3: Each group is responsible for assigning character parts and rehearsing its script. Once the group has agreed on character parts, each person underlines or highlights his/her assigned part(s) in the Reader's Theater.

Step 4: The group makes suggestions for improvements, additions, or changes to the presentation of the script. The teacher monitors by moving from group to group, encouraging and asking questions of the readers. Allow groups to practice between three to five times to become ready for an audience.

Step 5: Schedule group presentations. You may choose to do one per day or hold all of them on the same day. Students present their Reader's Theater to the other students in the class.

Adapting this Activity:

1. You might require the students to take the scripts home to do some home rehearsal. You could ask parents or other family members to sign on a signature card that the students practiced at home and/or you could ask the parents or family members to write the student two comments: a positive one and a wish that they would like the student to consider to improve his or her performance.

25 Ways to Add Interest to Reader's Theater

There are several things you can do to make your Reader's Theater presentations more interesting. Choose whatever you think your students would enjoy in order to add interest, focus, and attention to your presentations. Here are just a few to get you thinking:

1. Have students read character parts in unison. This can be done during practice or actually within the presentation to help students examine the feelings of each character and to better identify with the character.
2. Encourage dramatic student voice inflections in the reading.
3. Have students vary the tempo at which the characters speak during the reading.
4. Have the students moderate vocal intensity and verbal voice changes: loud voices, whispering, sad voices, excited voices, etc.
5. Brainstorm appropriate facial expressions that could be used with verbal wording.
6. Add seating and standing directions to the script so that students are not seated throughout the entire reading.
7. Use stage direction and wording typically used in dramatic acting:
   - "Stage right" refers to the reader's right.
   - "Stage left" refers to the reader's left.
   - "Upstage" refers to the area behind the readers.
   - "Downstage" refers to the area in front of the readers and in front of the audience.
8. Add reader entrances and exits into the script.
9. Have students add stage movements that they practice.
10. Add simple costume pieces to the scripts, like special hats or a handheld item.
11. Design some written signs that can be used during the presentation.
12. Make or use simple props to enhance the reading.
13. Add sound effects to the presentation.
14. Encourage eye contact with the audience and only occasionally with other cast members. (You want them to concentrate on the audience just like a storyteller does when he or she is telling a story.)
15. Have the characters add some controlled movements or mimes while they are speaking.
16. Have students add simple puppets to the character readings.
17. Have the readers concentrate on their reading, but have several other students perform a silent puppet show imitating what is occurring.
18. Have students wear half masks or hold paper plate masks near the front of their faces. (Just be sure it does not interfere with the audience's ability to clearly hear the readers.)

19. Add music or chants to the reading that can be pre-recorded and played or interjected into the reading, at which point the readers will "freeze" and then other students will come onto the stage to chant or to sing.

20. Draw or trace scenery or objects related to the story with colorful transparency pens on overhead transparencies. Have the overhead facing behind the readers on an overhead screen. As the readers tell the story, one person can quietly change the transparencies on the overhead projector, thereby changing the scenery or the visual seen by the audience behind the readers.

21. Think about the staging arrangement of the readers. Readers might be arranged in rows or a semicircle, standing up or sitting on high stools. Perhaps a variety of seating at different levels might be used by the characters, depending upon whether they are major or minor characters in the story. Narrators might be placed at one or both ends of the staging area with the characters placed in the center of the stage.

22. Readers might look straight out into the audience or at an angle. Or, perhaps the readers will look at each other.

23. Scene changes that involve jumps in time or place might be shown by a group freeze, followed by a collective shift or verbal notation by the narrator.

24. Characters might exit the Reader's Theater by turning their backs to the audience.

25. Characters might actually portray the action described in the story, moving around the stage like one sees in a play. Or, you might choose to have your readers demonstrate little stage movement, opting instead to have them mime small actions like making a telephone call or running in place (with little actual movement around the whole staging area).

Writing Scripts

There are no steadfast rules for how to write Reader's Theater scripts. What you find below are some suggestions that you may want to consider incorporating as you create scripts.

Front Page of Script:

Summary—A short summary gives the readers an overview of the plot.

Background—Have a section that provides some cultural or background information about the topic of the script. This section will activate any prior knowledge and help to build a background about new or unfamiliar topics.

Staging—This section might include some easy suggestions to help set the scene with some simple props or costumes the students may wish to incorporate.

Number and Names of Character Parts—This is a quick view of the name and number of characters in the script.

Vocabulary—This is a short list of new or unfamiliar vocabulary that is presented in the script. Words, pronunciation, and definitions are listed in this section.

Actual Script:

This is the heart of the Reader's Theater information. Usually this is a four- to six-page text that students will read during rehearsals and performances. These scripts contain a mix of narrator parts and character dialogue.

Teachers may write the script for the students OR they might have some students create the scripts for the Reader's Theater.

Activities:

You may wish to provide students with two or three pages of follow-up activities for them to work on when they have completed reading and practicing the script. These activities could be things that students can complete independently. That way, the teacher can provide individualized or small-group instruction or hold rehearsal with another group of students.

Your activities could relate to the script or novel you are reading. Or, you can assign some more general activities for students to work on. Here are some ideas of things to do in Spanish:

1. Original Story

Create your own original story from past vocabulary lists. It must contain at least 50 words and be completely in Spanish. Underline the words in the story from the vocabulary list you are using.

2. Picture Story

Draw at least seven pictures in a story format, using pieces of white, unlined paper that is available in class. Draw one picture per paper. Color each picture, using either colored pencils or crayons that are available in class. Under each picture, write at least two sentences, telling what is happening in each picture in Spanish. (You may have more than two sentences per page but not less than two sentences in Spanish.) The pictures must be related and tell a story.

3. Crossword Puzzle

Using your current or recent vocabulary list, make up a crossword puzzle, using at least 12 vocabulary words. Your clues should be written in Spanish, or they may be picture clues. No English may be used. Include an answer key.

4. POV Change

Take a story already done in class and rewrite it from a different point of view (POV) or perspective. For example, if the story was about a girl ("una chica" or "una muchacha"), tell the same story using "yo," "ellos," "ellas," "nosotros," or "noso-tras" forms. You may not use any story that was already used for POV changes in class but you are welcome to use the same story with a different POV change. Remember to make all the verb and pronoun changes needed and all other changes generated by the change in the POV.

5. Flashcards

Using your current vocabulary list, make a set of FANCY flashcards. You should make flashcards for at least 10 of the vocabulary words, with the Spanish word neatly written on one side and an attractive, colored picture on the other side. Use 3x5 or 4x6 index cards. Create a cover index card with your name, date, and identification of the vocabulary list. You need to paperclip the set together when the flashcards are done.

6. Pictionary

Make a list of 10 sentences from the current vocabulary list that could be used as Pictionary clues. Draw a simple illustration next to each sentence and color in the illustration.

7. New Ending

Take a story already done in class and write a different ending to it. Change what happens. Write at least 50 words in Spanish. Review the story in English at the top of the paper before you begin writing the new ending in Spanish for the story.

8. Crazy Commands

Write 10 crazy, but appropriate, commands that you could give to another student. Draw and color an illustration of each one of your crazy commands. Use white, unlined paper.

9. Sequel

Write a sequel to a story that has already been done in class. The sequel must have a minimum of 50 words. Be sure to specify which story you are using as a starting point.

10. "Opposites Poster"

Using white, unlined paper, draw at least five pairs of vocabulary words that are opposites. Illustrate the poster.

11. 20 Original Sentences

Write 20 original sentences in Spanish, using the vocabulary list presently being studied. Underline the words from the vocabulary list. The sentences do not need to make a story.

12. Comic Strip

Draw an original comic strip (at least five boxes) and write the script for it in Spanish (at least 35 words). It should be clever, amusing, and appropriate for school.

13. Vocabulary Test

Make a vocabulary test and key. It can be any format (multiple choice, matching, translation, etc.) as long as you use ALL the words in one of the vocabulary lists. It must include at least 20 words. Who knows, maybe I'll use it and you will know all the answers!

14. Poet

Write a poem in Spanish with at least 35 Spanish words in it.

15. Make a Game

Create a game of some sort, using a vocabulary list or list of review words. It can copy a game show, something that has been played in class, or it can be your own invention, but it needs to show originality.

16. Children's Storybook

Make up a children's storybook in Spanish. Use recent vocabulary. Your story should be at least 50 words long, and should contain six colored, illustrated pages. Staple the pages together in a "book fashion."

17. Word Search

Using your current vocabulary list, make a word search that contains at least 20 vocabulary words. Make a list of picture clues. Make sure to include an answer key as well as the puzzle.

18. Novel Review

Choose one "scene" from the current novel being read in class or a recent novel. On an unlined piece of white paper, draw a colored picture, collage, or other attractive visual image representing the scene, and then write 50 words in Spanish describing the picture.

19. Postcard

Pretend you are on vacation in a Spanish-speaking country. You choose the location. Make a postcard telling a friend about what you are seeing and doing during your vacation. You should write at least 50 words in Spanish and illustrate the postcard in a way that shows a positive aspect of the place you are visiting.

20. Make Up Your Own

Make up your own assignment, but get it approved first. It must include something to do with this class and must include at least 50 words in Spanish.

Differentiating Instruction in Reader's Theater

There are a number of ways you may wish to differentiate some portions of the Reader's Theater.

Beginning or low-level students:

1. Partner lower-level readers with stronger readers who read the same role together. The paired support often allows low-level students to participate completely in the Reader's Theater activities.
2. Give these students parts that have a repeating refrain.
3. Have these students take certain parts only after they have heard other students read the parts several times, so it is easier for them after hearing the repeated phrases.
4. Give students something that has a rhyme or a song/chant to help students to more easily read the materials.
5. Give low-level students an audio recording of the reading so that students can hear and practice lines at home or in another classroom.

Accelerated students:

1. Allow these students to write additional elaboration and parts on the original script.
2. Have these students create rhymes, chants, or songs for the scripts.
3. Allow these students to work together on a more difficult version of the script.
4. Challenge these students to create a more fully staged production by adding stage directions, props, and sets. They can also create new, or expanding existing, dialogue.
5. Use these students as directors to manage and run small group rehearsals in class.
6. Have these students change the scripts into other forms, such as poems, music, performing dance, small readers, or songs.
7. Have students make children's storybooks complete with illustrations and story booklet forms.

Resources, References, and Downloads

Online Resources

10 best apps for classroom participation (iPhone/iPad): Appcrawlr is a leading app search and discovery program offering lots of innovative features to provide users with the most relevant and trusted recommendations for searching and discovering apps. Go to http://appcrawlr.com/ios-apps/best-apps-class-participation

20 audio lessons that will teach you Spanish, French, Italian, and German: Download free lessons from iTunes or feeds from the websites. Podcasts are also available to download on cell phones. Go to http://www.openculture.com/freelanguagelessons

Curriculet: This tool allows you to build questions and comments into a reading that the students can access outside of the classroom. The students can communicate within the readings to respond to questions to help check understanding and comprehension of assignments. Go to www.curriculet.com

Classroom clip art: From elementary cartoons to illustrations and photographs of live culture, this site offers clip art in a categorized gallery. Go to http://classroomclipart.com/

Designing presentational performance tasks and their rubrics: ACTFL (American Council for the Teaching of Foreign Languages) webinar that defines presentational communication and gives advice for creating presentational performance assessments and rubrics to evaluate them. Go to http://www.visualwebcaster.com/imageSlides/76730/ACTFL%20Webinar%20Series-Presentational%20Tasks-Apr%202011%20[Compatibility%20Mode].pdf

Duolingo: Duolingo is a free language-learning website and crowdsourced text translation platform. The service is designed so that as users progress through the lessons, they simultaneously help to translate websites and other documents. It is a way that teachers can provide an additional language-learning source to their students, and once each lesson is completed, students read authentic sources and complete activities on the internet from authentic web-based sources. Go to https://www.duolingo.com/

FL Teach: Foreign language-teaching forum that offers lesson plans and web links to teachers in a variety of world languages. Go to http://flteach.org/

Foreign language-teaching methods: A stand-alone classroom methods course that guides teachers to implementing 12 modules in the language classroom: speaking, writing, listening, reading, vocabulary, grammar, pragmatics, culture, the language learner, classroom management, technology, and assessment. Sample lesson plans and practical ideas for classroom application are offered in each module. Go to http://coerll.utexas.edu/methods/

World language vocabulary, grammar, and readings: LanguageGuide.org is an online language-learning resource available in numerous languages, including English, Spanish, French, Portuguese, Italian, German, Dutch, Turkish, Arabic, Russian, Mandarin, Japanese, and Korean. This illustrated vocabulary guide contains sound-integrated exercises at three levels (beginner, intermediate, and advanced) and allows for independent practice at the learner's own pace. These practice exercises are appropriate for elementary and middle school students, and this resource would be well suited for a teacher webpage. Thematic topics vary by language but generally include numbers, parts of the body, clothing, food, animals, weather, home, and school. There is an option menu on each screen for listening, speaking, and reading practice, as well as a quiz for students to check their comprehension. Some languages also feature a "grammar and readings" section for more advanced learners. Go to http://www.languageguide.org/

Free Technology for Teachers: This is a great site to find out what's new in technology for our use. The purpose of this site is to share information about free resources that teachers can use in their classrooms. In 2008, Free Technology for Teachers was awarded the Edublogs Award for "Best Resource Sharing Blog." In 2009, Free Technology for Teachers was again awarded the Edublogs Award for "Best Resource Sharing Blog" and was awarded the Edublogs Award for "Best Individual Blog." In 2010, Free Technology for Teachers was awarded the Edublogs Awards for "Best Resource Sharing Blog," "Best Ed Tech Support," and "Best Individual Blog."

In 2011, Free Technology for Teachers received the Edublogs Award for "Best Ed Tech Blog."

Also presented on this site are links to learning languages, activities, and image-based language lessons. Go to http://www.freetech4teachers.com/

Google apps in classrooms and schools: A slideshow that offers 32 ways to use Google apps in the classroom. Provides ideas, demonstrations, examples of projects, and links to additional resources. Go to https://docs.google.com/presentation/d/1_6fh7wXkugHQbbA 2ILrjsFqysvclJCbul2I3Oc912D8/present#slide=id.i0

Graphic organizers: Offers many kinds of graphic organizers that work with a variety of literacy techniques. The first link contains many graphic organizers in Spanish. Go to http://www.proteacher.com/020067.shtml

ICDL—International Children's Digital Library: This site has a wonderful collection of children's books from all over the world. Go to http://en.childrenslibrary.org/

Lingro—the coolest dictionary known to hombre: Lingro is an online dictionary tool that allows users to link all words for any URL address or uploaded document to the available dictionaries in 11 languages. Once the URL address or document is linked to the Lingro dictionaries every word becomes "clickable" and is linked to the program's dictionary to view either a definition in English or a translation in the other languages. This site can be used by world language teachers and students in a variety of ways to encourage reading comprehension in L2. For teachers' use, Lingro can be used to create guided practice activities with L2 readings, such as in an online newspaper or uploaded document. The teacher guides students through the target vocabulary to be learned and promotes the discussion of its context use and correct translation. For student use, vocabulary lists can be created with the click of a button, which can later be reviewed as flashcards or word lists with examples of use in contextual sentences. This tool aids learners by providing a quick reference for vocabulary definitions, thereby negating the need to interrupt a lesson or reading exercise for lengthy amounts of time. Go to http://lingro.com/

Resources and ideas for language teachers: Offers in list format a variety of resources from which teachers can create lessons, including: YouTube videos, PowerPoint, activity sheets, readings, comics, and foreign news. Go to http://neiljones.org/

Storybird—artful storytelling: Storybird is a visual storytelling community; i.e., a global hub of readers, writers, and artists of all ages. Students and teachers can make, read, and share short, visual stories with an easy-to-use tool. Teachers and students can select artwork, drag and organize photos, and add their own text to create beautiful digital stories. These creations can then be published on the web with adjustable privacy settings and with the option to allow comments, which is perfect for teachers to encourage student collaboration. In addition, there is the option to create a classroom account. You can sign up for free or consider an upgrade to a paid account. World language teachers can create stories for their students to read and share online. Students can also read or create short visual stories to share with their teacher and their peers. Go to http://storybird.com/

MFL—Storybirds: Here are sample Storybirds (see item above) in different languages. Go to http://mfl-storybirds.wikispaces.com

Teach-nology world language lesson plans: Pre-made lesson plans (many with virtual components) for all levels. Go to http://www.teach-nology.com/teachers/lesson_plans/languages/

WordTalk: This is a free text-to-speech plug-in for Microsoft Word. It will verbalize the text of the document and highlight it as the program runs. It contains a talking dictionary and a text-to-mp3 converter that can be used with languages other than English. Go to http://www.wordtalk.org.uk/Home

References

Adams, M. J., & Bruck, M. (1993). Word recognition: The interface of educational policies and scientific research. *Reading and Writing: An Interdisciplinary Journal, 5,* 113–139.

Ajideh, P. (2006). Schema-theory based considerations on pre-reading activities in ESP textbooks. *The Asian EFL Journal Teaching Articles, 16,* 1–19.

Allen, J. (1999). *Words, words, words: Teaching vocabulary in grades 4–12.* Portland, MA: Stenhouse Publishers.

Anderson, M. H. (1994). Developing active readers: A pedagogical framework for second language reading class. *System, 22,* 177–194.

Anderson, N. J. (1999). *Exploring second language reading: Issues and strategies.* Boston, MA: Heinle & Heinle.

Anderson, R. C. (1996). *Research foundations for wide reading.* Urbana, IL: Center for the Study of Reading, Special Invitational Conference.

Anderson, R. C., & Nagy, W. (1991). Word meanings. In R. Barr, M. Kamil, P. Monsenthal, & P. D. Pearson (Eds.), *Handbook of reading research* (pp. 690–724). New York: Longman.

Anderson, R. C., & Nagy, W. E. (1992). The vocabulary conundrum. *American Educator, 16*(4), 14–19, 44–47.

Armbruster, B. B., & Nagy, W. E. (1992). Vocabulary in content area lessons. *The Reading Teacher, 45*(7), 550–551.

Baumann, J. F., & Kameenui, E. J. (1991). Research on vocabulary instruction: Ode to Voltaire. In J. Flood, J. J. Lapp, & J. R. Squire (Eds.), *Handbook of research on teaching the English language arts* (pp. 604–632). New York: MacMillan.

Beck, I. L., & McKeown, M. G. (1991). Conditions of vocabulary acquisition. In P. D. Pearson (Ed.), *The handbook of reading research* (Vol. 2, pp. 789–814). New York: Longman Press.

Becker, W. C. (1977). Teaching and reading language to the disadvantaged: What we have learned from field research. *Harvard Educational Review, 47,* 518–543.

Billmeyer, R., & Barton, M. L. (1998). *Teaching reading in the content areas: If not me, then who?* Aurora, CO: Mid-Continent Research for Education and Learning.

Blachowicz, C.L. (1986). Making connections: Alternatives to the vocabulary notebook. *Journal of Reading, 29*(2), 643–649.

Block, C. (1997). *Literacy difficulties: Diagnosis and instruction*. San Diego: Harcourt Brace.

Block, C.C., Gambrell, L.B., & Pressley, M. (2002). *Improving comprehension: Rethinking research, theory, and classroom practice*. San Francisco: Jossey-Bass.

Block, C.C., & Pressley, M. (2002). *Comprehension instruction: Research-based best practices*. New York: Guilford.

Blum, I., Koskinen, P.A., Tennant, N., Parker, E.M., Straub, M., & Curry, C. (1995). Using audiotaped books to extend classroom literacy instruction into the homes of second-language learners. *Journal of Reading Behavior, 27*, 535–563.

Buehl, D. (1995). *Classroom strategies for interactive learning*. Schofield, WI: Wisconsin State Reading Association Monograph.

Cho, K.S., Ahn, K.O., & Krashen, S. (2005). The effects of narrow reading of authentic texts on interest and reading ability in English as a foreign language. *Reading Improvement, 42*, 58–64.

Clay, M.M. (2002). *An observational survey of early literacy achievement*. Portsmouth, NH: Heinemann.

Coady, J. (1997). L2 vocabulary acquisition through extensive reading. In J. Coady & T. Huckin (Eds.), *Second language vocabulary acquisition: A rationale for pedagogy* (pp. 174–200). Cambridge, UK: Cambridge University Press.

Collins, A., Brown, J.S., & Newman, S.E. (1989). Cognitive apprenticeship: Teaching the crafts of reading, writing, and mathematics. In L.B. Resnick (Ed.), *Knowing, learning, and instruction: Essays in honor of Robert Glaser* (pp. 453–494). Hillsdale, NJ: Erlbaum.

Cowan, G., & Cowan, E. (1980). *Writing*. New York: Wiley.

Cubing. Retrieved July 23, 2008 from the Curry University of Virginia website: http://curry. edschool.virginia.edu/files/nagc_cubing__think_dots.pdf.

Cunningham, A.E., & Stanovich, K.E. (2003). Reading matters: How reading engagement influences cognition. In J. Flood, D. Lapp, J.R. Squire, & J.M. Jensen (Eds.), *Handbook of research on teaching the English language arts* (2nd ed.). Mahwah, NJ: Erlbaum.

Davey, B. (1983). Think aloud—modeling the cognitive processes of reading comprehension. *Journal of Reading, 27*, 44–47.

Day, R. (1994, January–March). Selecting a passage for the EFL reading class. *English Teaching Forum, 32*(1), 20.

Day, R.R., & Bamford, J. (1998). *Extensive reading in the second language classroom*. New York: Cambridge University Press.

Day, R.R., & Bamford, J. (2002). Top ten principles for teaching extensive reading. *Reading in a Foreign Language, 14*, 136–141.

Day, R., Omura, C., & Hiramatsu, M. (1991). Incidental EFL vocabulary learning and reading. *Reading in a Foreign Language, 7*, 541–551.

Derin, A., & Gokce, K. (2006, December). Elementary school EFL learners' vocabulary learning: The effects of post-reading activities. *Canadian Modern Language Review, 63*(2), 255–273.

Dole, I., Duffy, G., Roehler, L., & Pearson, P. D. (1991). Moving from the old to the new: Research on reading comprehension instruction. *Review of Educational Research, 61*, 239–264.

Ellery, V. (2005). *Creating strategic readers: Techniques for developing competency in phonemic awareness, phonics, fluency, vocabulary, and comprehension*. Newark, DE: International Reading Association.

Elley, W. B. (1989). Vocabulary acquisition from listening to stories. *Reading Research Quarterly, 24*(2), 174–187.

Elley, W. B. (1991). Acquiring literacy in second language: The effect of book-based programs. *Language Learning, 41*(3), 375–411.

Faulkner, H. J., & Levy, B. A. (1994). How text difficulty and reader skill interact to produce differential reliance on work and content overlap in reading transfer. *Journal of Experimental Child Psychology, 50*, 1–24.

Fielding, L., & Pearson, P. D. (1994). Reading comprehension: What works? *Educational Leadership, 51*(5), 62–67.

Forbes, S., & Briggs, C. (Eds.). (2003). *Research in reading recovery, vol. II*. Portsmouth, NJ: Heinemann.

Fuchs, L. S., Fuchs, D., Hosp, M. K., & Jenkins, J. (2001). Oral reading fluency as an indicator of reading competence: A theoretical, empirical, and historical analysis. *Scientific Studies of Reading, 5*(3), 239–256.

Grabe, W. (1991). Current developments in second language reading research. *TESOL Quarterly, 25*(3), 375–406.

Grabe, W. (2004). Research on teaching reading. *Annual Review of Applied Linguistics, 24*, 44–69.

Graves, M. F. (1986). Vocabulary learning and instruction. In E. Z. Rothkopf (Ed.), *Review of Research in Education, 13*, 49–89.

Green, M. (1998). Rapid retrieval of information: Reading aloud with a purpose. *Journal of Adolescent and Adult Literacy, 41*, 306–307.

Hafiz, F. M., & Tudor, I. (1990). Graded readers as an input medium in L2 learning. *System, 18*(1), 31–42.

Hall, T., & Strangman, N. (2002). *Graphic organizers*. Wakefield, MA: National Center on Accessing the General Curriculum. Retrieved March 10, 2009 from Center for

Applied Special Technology Universal Design for Learning website: http://www.cast.org/publications/ncac/ncac_go.html.

Hoover, W.A., & Gough, P. B. (n.d.). *Reading acquisition framework*. Retrieved February 2009 from the Southwest Educational Development Laboratory website: http://www.sedl.org/reading/topics/myths.pdf.

Johns, J., & Lenski, S. (1997). *Improving reading: A handbook of strategies*. Dubuque, IA: Kendall Hunt.

Jones, B. F., Palincsar, A. S., Ogle, D. S., & Carr, E. G. (1987). *Strategic teaching learning: Cognitive instruction in the content areas*. Elmhurst, IL: Association for Supervision and Curriculum Development and North Central Regional Educational Laboratory.

Kagan, S. (1992). *Cooperative learning*. San Clemente, CA: Resources for Teachers Inc.

Keene, E. O., & Zimmerman, S. (1997). *Mosaic of thought: Teaching comprehension in a reader's workshop*. Portsmouth, NH: Heinemann.

Knight, S. (1994). Dictionary use while reading: The effects on comprehension and vocabulary acquisition for students of different verbal abilities. *The Modern Language Journal, 78*, 285–299.

Koskinen, P. S., & Blum, I. H. (1984). Repeated oral reading and the acquisition of fluency. In J. Niles & L. Harris (Eds.), *Changing perspectives on research in reading, language processing and instruction* (pp. 183–187). Rochester, NY: National Reading Conference.

Koyama, T., & Takeuchi, O. (2004). How look up frequency affects EFL learning: An empirical study on the use of handheld-electronic dictionaries. *Proceedings of CLaSIC 2004*, 1018–1024. Retrieved March 10, 2009 from http://www.paccall.org/2004/2004proceedings_papers/koyama.pdf.

Krashen, S. D. (1989). We acquire vocabulary and spelling by reading: Additional evidence for the input hypothesis. *The Modern Language Journal, 73*, 440–464.

Krashen, S. D. (1995). Free voluntary reading: Linguistic and affective arguments and some new applications. In F. Eckman, D. Highland, P. Lee, J. Mileham, & R. Weber (Eds.), *Second language acquisition theory and pedagogy* (pp. 187–202). Mahwah, NJ: Lawrence Erlbaum Associates.

Krashen, S. D. (2004). *The power of reading: Insights from the research*. Portsmouth, NH: Heinemann.

Krashen, S. D., & McQuillan, J. (2007, October). The case for late intervention. *Educational Leadership, 62*(2), 68–72.

LaBerge, D., & Samuels, S. J. (1974). Toward a theory of automatic information processing in reading. *Cognitive Psychology, 6*, 293–323.

Laflamme, J. G. (1997). The effect of the Multiple Exposure Vocabulary Method and the Target Reading/Writing Strategy on test scores. *Journal of Adolescent and Adult Literacy, 40*(5), 372–381.

Langenberg, D. N. (Ed.). (2000). *Report of the National Reading Panel: Teaching children to read*. Washington, DC: U.S. Department of Health and Human Services.

Liberman, A. M. (1992). The relation of speech to reading and writing. In R. Frost & L. Katz (Eds.), *Orthography, phonology, morphology, and meaning* (pp. 167–178). Amsterdam: North-Holland.

Little, M. (2007). *Best practices toolkit: Graphic organizers*. Evanston, IL: Houghton Mifflin Company.

Long, S. P., Winograd, P., & Bridge, C. (1989). The effects of reader and text characteristics on reports of imagery during and after reading. *Reading Research Quarterly, 24*, 353–372.

Lyman, F. (1981). The responsive classroom discussion. In A. S. Anderson (Ed.), *Mainstreaming digest* (pp. 109–113). College Park, MD: University of Maryland College of Education.

Marzano, R., Pickering, D., & Pollock, J. E. (2001). *Classroom instruction that works: Research based strategies for increasing student achievement*. Alexandria, VA: ASCD.

McTighe, J., & Wiggins, G. (2004). *Understanding by design professional development workbook*. Alexandria, VA: Association for Supervision and Curriculum Development.

Moats, L. C. (1999). *Teaching reading is rocket science* [Item #372]. Washington, DC: American Federation of Teachers.

Nagy, W. E. (1997). On the role of context in first- and second-language vocabulary learning. In N. Schmitt & M. McCarthy (Eds.), *Vocabulary: Description, acquisition and pedagogy* (pp. 64–83). Cambridge, UK: Cambridge University Press.

Nagy, W. E., Anderson, R. C., & Herman, P. A. (1987). Learning word meanings from context during normal reading. *American Educational Research Journal, 24*, 237–270.

Nagy, W. E., & Herman, P. (1985). Incidental vs. instructional approaches to increasing reading vocabulary. *Educational Perspectives, 23*, 16–21.

Nagy, W. E., & Herman, P. (1987). Breadth and depth of vocabulary knowledge: Implications for acquisition and instruction. In M. McKeown & M. Curtis (Eds.), *The nature of vocabulary acquisition* (pp. 19–35). Hillsdale, NJ: Lawrence Erlbaum.

Nation, I.S.P. (1997). The language learning benefits of extensive reading. *The Language Teacher, 21*(5), 13–16.

National Reading Panel. (2000). *The report of the national reading panel: Teaching children to read. An evidence-based assessment of the scientific research literature on reading and its implications for reading instruction*. Washington, DC: National Reading Panel.

Oczuks, L. (2003). *Reciprocal teaching at work: Strategies for improving reading comprehension*. Newark, DE: International Reading Association.

Ogle, D. M. (1986). K-W-L: A teaching model that develops active reading of expository text. *Reading Teacher, 39*, 564–570.

Palincsar, A.S., & Brown, A. (1984). Reciprocal teaching of comprehension-fostering and comprehension monitoring activities. *Cognition and Instruction, 1*(2), 117–175.

Palincsar, A.S., & Brown, A.L. (1985). Reciprocal teaching: Activities to promote read(ing) with your mind. In T.L. Harris & E.J. Cooper (Eds.), *Reading, thinking and concept development: Strategies for the classroom*. New York: The College Board.

Pearson, P.D., Dole, J.A., Duffy, G.G., & Roehler, L.R. (1992). Developing expertise in reading comprehension: What should be taught and how should it be taught? In J. Farstup & S.J. Samuels (Eds.), *What research should be taught and how should it be taught*. Newark, DE: International Reading Association.

Pearson, P.D., & Gallagher, M. (1983). The instruction of reading comprehension. *Contemporary Educational Psychology, 8*, 317–344.

Pigada, M., & Schmitt, N. (2006). Vocabulary acquisition from extensive reading: A case study. *Reading in a Foreign Language, 18*, 1–28.

Pinnell, G.S., & Fountas, I.C. (1998). *Word matters: Teaching phonics and spelling in the reading/writing classroom*. Portsmouth, NJ: Heinemann.

Pinnell, G.S., Pikulski, J.J., Wixson, K.K., Campbell, J.R., Gough, P.B., & Beatty, A.S. (1995). *Listening to children read aloud data from NAEP's integral reading performance record CIRPR at grade 4*. Washington, DC: Office of Educational Research and Improvement, U.S. Department of Education.

Pressley, M., & Wharton-McDonald, R. (1997). Skilled comprehension and its development through instruction. *School Psychology Review, 26*(3), 448–467.

Rashotte, C.A., & Torgesen, J.K. (1985). Repeated reading and reading fluency in learning disabled children. *Reading Research Quarterly, 20*, 180–188.

Rasinski, T.V., Padak, N., Linek, W., & Sturtevant, E. (1994). The effects of fluency development instruction on urban second grade readers. *Journal of Education Research, 87*, 158–164.

Rayner, K. (1998). Eye movement in reading and informational processing: Twenty years of research. *Psychological Bulletin, 124*, 372–422.

Richardson, J.S., & Morgan, R.F. (1994). *Reading to learn in the content areas*. Belmont, CA: Wadsworth.

Robb, L. (1997). Stretch your students' reading vocabulary. *Instructor, 106*(8), 34.

Rosenshine, B.V. (1980). Skill hierarchies in reading comprehension. In. R.J. Spiro, B.C. Bruce, & W.F. Brewer (Eds.), *Theoretical issues in reading comprehension* (pp. 535–559). Hillsdale, NJ: Lawrence Erlbaum Associates.

Routeman, R. (2003). *Reading essentials: The specifics you need to teach reading well*. Portsmouth, NH: Heinemann.

Ruddell, R., Ruddell, M., & Singer, H. (1994). *Theoretical models and processes of reading*. Newark, DE: International Reading Association.

Ruddell, R. B., & Unrau, N. (2004). *Theoretical models and processes of reading*. Newark, DE: International Reading Association.

Samuels, S. J. (1979). The method of repeated readings. *The Reading Teacher, 32*, 403–408.

Schmitt, N., & Carter, R. (2000). The lexical advantages of narrow reading for second language learners. *TESOL Journal, 9*(1), 4–9.

Sherman, S. (1991, November 18). America won't win till it reads more. *Fortune*. Retrieved February 22, 2009 from http://money.cnn.com/magazines/fortune/fortune_archive/1991/11/18/75745/index.htm.

Shu, H., Anderson, R. C., & Zhang, H. (1995). Incidental learning of word meanings while reading: A Chinese and American cross-cultural study. *Reading Research Quarterly, 30*(1), 76–95.

Snow, C. E., Burns, S. M., & Griffin, P. (1998). *Preventing reading difficulties in young children*. Washington, DC: National Academy Press.

Sousa, D. A. (2001). *How the brain learns* (2nd ed.). Thousand Oaks, CA: Corwin Press.

Sulzby, E., & Teale, W. H. (1991). Emergent literacy. In R. Barr, M. L. Kamil, P. Mosenthal, & P. D. Pearson (Eds.), *Handbook of reading research* (pp. 727–757). New York: Longman.

Taguchi, E., & Gorsuch, G. J. (2002). Transfer effects of repeated EFL reading on reading new passages: A preliminary investigation. *Reading in a Foreign Language, 14*(1), 43–65.

Taguchi, E., Takayasu-Maass, M., & Gorsuch, G. J. (October 2004). Developing reading fluency in EFL: How assisted repeated reading and extensive reading affect fluency development. *Reading in a Foreign Language, 16*(2), 70–96.

ToonDoo comic strip creator. Retrieved February 24, 2008 from Jambav website: http://www.toondoo.com/toondoo/Home.toon.

Topping, K. (1987). Paired reading: A powerful technique for parent use. *The Reading Teacher, 40*, 608–614.

Tsang, W. (1996). Comparing the effects of reading and writing on writing performance. *Applied Linguistics, 17*(2), 210–233.

Waring, R., & Takaki, M. (2003). At what rate do learners learn and retain new vocabulary from reading a graded reader? *Reading in a Foreign Language, 15*, 130–163.

White, T. G., Graves, M. F., & Slater, W. H. (1990). Growth of reading vocabulary in diverse elementary schools: Decoding and word meaning. *Journal of Educational Psychology, 82*(2), 281–290.

Wood, K., & Muth, K. D. (1991). The case for improved instruction in the middle grades. *Journal of Reading, 35*, 84–89.

Wren, S. (n.d.). *The cognitive foundations of learning to read: A framework*. Austin, TX: Southwest Educational Development Laboratory.

Young, A. R., Bowers, P. G., & MacKinnon, G. E. (1996). Effects of prosodic modeling and repeated reading on poor readers' fluency and comprehension. *Applied Psycholinguistics*, *17*, 59–84.

Zygouris-Coe, V., Wiggins, M. B., & Smith, L. H. (2004). Engaging students with text: The 3-2-1 strategy. The Reading Teacher, *58*(4), 381–384.

Appendix

Strategy 1: Annolighting the Text

Reader's Text with Highlights	Annotations

Strategy 5: Bloom's Taxonomy Questions

	Questions About the Text	*Answers to Questions*
"Knowledge"—the recall of specific information		
"Comprehension"—an understanding of what was read		
"Application"—the converting of abstract content to concrete situations		
"Analysis"—the comparison and contrast of the content to personal experiences		
"Synthesis"—the organization of thoughts, ideas, and information from the content		
"Evaluation"—the judgment and evaluation of characters, actions, and outcome for personal reflection and understanding		

Strategy 9: "Five W's and an H"

Example:

	Questions About the Text	*Answers to Questions*
"Who"		
"What"		
"Where"		
"When"		
"Why"		
"How"		

Strategy 15: KWL Chart

What do I Know?	What do I Want to Know?	What did I Learn?

Strategy 20: Predicting ABCs

Predicting ABCs

Skill: Previewing Vocabulary

A-B	C-D	E-F	G-I
J-K	**L-LL**	**M-N**	**O-P**
Q-R	**S-T**	**U-W**	**X-Z**

Strategy 23: Say, Mean, Matter

SAY	MEAN	MATTER
What does the text say?	What does the author mean?	Why does it matter to me or others?
What happened?	How do I interpret this?	Why is this important?
Cite text (quotation) or paraphrase.	Read "between the lines."	What is the significance?
		What are the implications?

Strategy 26: Story Mapping

Information for the Teacher	Directions for the Student
Setting: Writers let the reader know where and when the story takes place.	Filling in the three pieces of information about the setting of the story. 1. 2. 3. Information that shows WHEN this story happened: Information that shows WHERE this story took place: In WHAT PLACES did this story take place:
Characters: All stories have characters. They may be people, animals, or objects that the writer uses to tell the story.	Write the names of the characters found in the story and identify something the author has written about the character. Character's Name—Tell something the author has written about this character _____. 1. 2. 3. 4. 5.

Problem/Goal: Stories have action. The writer usually tells the reader about the characters and the problems they face with actions characters use to deal with their problems.	What was the first problem encountered in the book? How did the character(s) deal with the problem? Is there another problem encountered in the book? How did the character(s) deal with the problem?
Key Episodes: In a story, key events occur throughout the story.	List the key events that happen in the story. List them in the order that they happened from the beginning to the end of the reading. 1. 2. 3. 4. 5. 6. 7. 8.

Resolution/Outcome: In a story, the reader needs to determine if the problem was resolved and/or if the character's goal was met.	Describe the resolution or outcome of the story:
Theme: This is the "so what?" of a story map. This is the personal truth or universal truth; as in the larger meaning or importance.	Write a sentence or two about the conclusion explaining how things worked out for the characters:

Strategy 28: Textbook Activity Guide (TAG)

Here's an example of what a study guide might look like:

PP	Predict with partner
RDP	Read information silently and discuss with partner
SKDP	Skim silently by reading quickly and discuss with partner
RR	Read information silently and retell with partner (verbally or written form)
WR	Write an individual response
WRDP	Write an individual response and discuss with partner
MCO	Make a map, chart, or outline of information

1. _____ **PP**	[Note the page numbers here.] Survey the title, pictures, and headings for this chapter. After you discuss ideas with your partner, write down what you think you will learn in this chapter.
2. _____ **RDP**	[Note page numbers here.] Do the first three paragraphs on these pages.
3. _____ **SKDP**	[Note page numbers here.] Skim these pages to define the author's purpose in telling the reader this information.
4. _____ **RR**	[Note the page numbers here.] Retell with your partner, first verbally, what you have learned in this section. Then, retell in writing what you have learned.

5. _____ **WR**	[Note the page numbers here.] As you are reading, jot down key words in this section and write down definitions if you know what these words mean.
6. _____ **WRDP**	[Note the page numbers here.] Read these first four paragraphs and write a short summary on the main ideas found in this selection.
7. _____ **MCO**	Map: [Note the page number here]. Draw a map as a visual representation of the information on this page.

Self-Monitoring Check

Name: _____ **Class:** _____

After completing the TAG strategy with my partner on this text selection:

_____ I understand the information.

_____ I'm not sure that I understand the information.

_____ I do not understand the information and I need to restudy the information.

Strategy 32: Three-Two-One (3-2-1)

3 THINGS YOU FOUND OUT

1.

2.

3.

2 INTERESTING THINGS

1.

2.

1 QUESTION YOU STILL HAVE

1.

Strategy 34: Vocabulary Builder

Vocabulary Word

[Students write the new target vocabulary word here.]

Definition

[Students write the definition of the
vocabulary word in the target language.]

_____

_____

_____

_____

Student Visual Picture

_____

Antonyms/Synonyms

_____   _____

_____   _____

_____   _____

Sentence

[Students use the new target vocabulary word
in a sentence in the foreign language]

_____

_____

_____

_____

Strategy 35: Vocabulary Prediction Chart

Vocabulary Word	Predicted Meaning	After Reading Definition	Clue Words and Corresponding Page Numbers of Clue Words from the Text

Activity 8: Inference Boxes

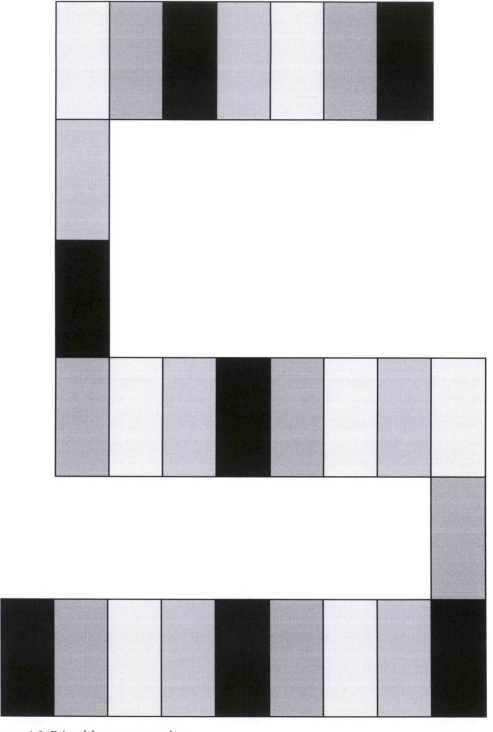

Figure 4.2 Printable game template

Activity 21: Tic-Tac-Toe Choice Board

Sample choice board:

Translate to Spanish.	*Translate to English.*	*Draw the meaning of the story detail.*
Circle the word that does not belong.	*Translate to Spanish aloud with a partner.*	*True or False?*
Unscramble the following phrases from the story vocabulary.	*¿Cómo se dice en inglés:*	*Identify the grammar mistakes in the following phrases.*